Higher Hopes:
A Black Man's Guide to College

By R. D. Smith

D0094193

Cover Art: *Still I Rise* by Kamal Mateen
reprinted with the permission of Solid
Inspiration Publishing. © Solid Inspiration
Publishing

First Printing, 2012

ISBN: 978-0615675091

BFI Technology LLC
P.O. Box 10051
Rochester, NY 14610

Table of Contents

Introduction 7

Chapter 1 Introspection 13

Chapter 2 Academics 19

Chapter 3 Finances... 65

Chapter 4 Relationships 97

Chapter 5 Health and Safety 137

Chapter 6 Extracurricular Activities................... 185

Chapter 7 Studying Abroad 205

Chapter 8 Transportation................................... 221

Chapter 9 Race and Class 231

Chapter 10 Technology 243

Chapter 11 Career 271

Concluding Remarks... 287

About the Author 289

Index.. 291

To all those striving to accomplish what our ancestors only dreamed of, and to my wife, Melissa, my brother and family for their constant support and comments.

Introduction

So you've made it.

Through the trials and tribulations of puberty, chemistry class, sports, and tons of extracurricular activities you've finally passed through the gauntlet known as high school. Congratulations. Of course after all of that, it can only get easier, right?

Of course it doesn't. The new path before you is filled with more challenges than high school, yet it also presents many more rewards as well.

Several things are about to hit you if they haven't already. First, you are now a legal adult in every way except legally drinking alcohol. That means no more excuses about "only being a kid," being able to vote in elections, and possibly serving in the armed forces. Second, you are being asked what you want to do with your life. If you are used to throwing out any half-baked answer that sounds good, that's fine, but in college you're going to have to start taking concrete steps to reach this goal so it becomes much more real. Granted, everyone has time to evolve on the journey, but the journey is rapidly quickening in pace. Third, you likely are about to face the first real independence from your parents.

All of this produces a lot of reactions, including pride, excitement, fear, and uncertainty. This could be the first big "next step" in your life you have actually had a say in. More to the point, once you step on the campus your first semester, it's all up to you.

There are a lot of college-prep books out there, and many of them are pretty good. Given that, it is probably a legitimate question why there needs to be another, specifically addressed to Black men. Or to pose the question differently, what does this book add that makes it worthwhile to its target audience versus a run-of-the-mill offering?

First, this confronts some of the specific issues that face Black males on campus that other guides may only address in a short or superficial manner. Second, I believe it can be helpful to target a group whose average performance in college could be much improved and I believe falls far short of its potential.

One measure of this is college participation. Though it has edged up over the decades, Black male college participation has basically flatlined, while still being at a relatively lower percentage. Women of all ethnic groups, in fact, now outnumber men in college participation rates, which is the percentage of people aged eighteen to twenty-four in college.

Since this is a guide for college students, you are assumed to already be part of the thirty percent or so who will be attending. Despite being a success getting into college, you cannot rest on your laurels. First, given the relatively lower participation rate, yield becomes much more important in producing college graduates in the Black community. A higher dropout rate combined with a lower participation rate seriously limits the pool of the college educated.

In addition, the combination of increasing competition for school admissions, both from the United States and abroad, the decline of affirmative action, and still poorly performing schools for many are putting pressure on even the current participation rate.

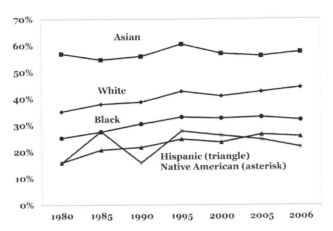

FIGURE 1: College participation since 1980 by race
(Census CPS October Supplement by year)

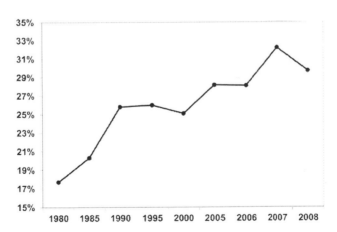

FIGURE 2: Black male college participation since 1980

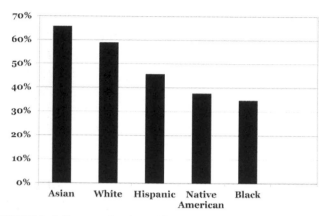

FIGURE 3: College graduation within 6-years by race for males (U.S. Department of Education, National Center for Education Statistics)

While I can't solve or even explain the source of all these issues, I do believe it should be the mission of everyone who attends college to first ask themselves if this is where they want or need to be, and if so, how they are going to succeed. If you can't do both of these, your time and money is better spent elsewhere. I assume if you are reading this book you can answer yes to the first question and want to have a plan for the second.

In addition, I wanted to write this book in order to help spread some of the knowledge I learned to succeed in my own college career over a decade ago. A lot of what is in this book may seem like common sense and not worth restating. A lot of this will be told to you by your parents or guardians, teachers, or administrators. Some of what I say will be controversial for some since I have a relatively take-no-prisoners attitude toward the type of destructive behavior that some people engage in as part of the "authentic" college experience.

You are free to accept or reject any of the advice contained in this book. I will touch upon all of the major facets of college—from academics to relationships to health and safety to finances and career. This book is not encyclopedic, so I will not claim to address every issue on every topic. In addition, this is not a detailed how-to book on many essential skills that will be discussed such as dating and finding the right career. There are specialized books that address these topics in detail, and I would recommend that the curious seek more information on the issues that are not covered comprehensively here.

In addition, I am speaking mostly from my own experience and those of my college friends. Therefore, there are some important areas I won't cover in detail since I don't think my insights are as informed as they could be given I have little experience in these matters. These include fraternities, which I did not pledge during my college time, and things such as the LGBT lifestyle in college. The most important thing you must learn though is college is and will be what you make of it. Unless you are living at or near home, your parents will not always be there and the school and its administrators typically do not feel it is their responsibility to hold your hand or make sure you are happy at all times. There are several things you need that will be repeated over and over including a vision, a support group (family, peers, mentors, administrators), and to keep healthy and financially sound.

One final note is that despite a lot of the doom and gloom out there, many young Black men are doing well and making the right decisions. One common erroneous statistic that keeps being repeated is that there are more Black men in prison than college. Well, yes and no. Yes, if you compare all Black men of ALL age groups with the number of 18-24 year olds in college. Though this statistic is indeed sobering and depressing the issue is that you have to ask yourself, how many opportunities does someone over 24 have for college versus going to prison? A big bump in this number is that 7.3% of Black males 30-34 are incarcerated in state and federal prison (Department of Justice, Prisoners in 2010 report). Looking at the 18-24 age group though, 27.9% of Black males 18-24 were in college according to stats from the Department of Education. The same statistic for prisoners aged 18-24 (in 2010) was between 3-4% with a high of 4.6% for the 20-24 age group according to the Department of Justice Prisoners in 2010 data report.

It is important to remember that the right to attend the college of your choice is very new for the Black community. Significant numbers of people fought, had their lives destroyed, or were even killed to give you this opportunity. Therefore, try to keep this in mind the next time you don't want to study "just cause".

Chapter 1
Introspection

Hence the saying: If you know the enemy and know yourself, you need not fear the result of a hundred battles. If you know yourself but not the enemy, for every victory gained you will also suffer a defeat. If you know neither the enemy nor yourself, you will succumb in every battle.
—Sun Tzu, The Art of War

So you are at college or soon will be there. This is the culmination of a massive amount of effort throughout high school—sports, extracurricular activities, PSAT, SAT or ACT, hours of dense applications, nail biting about early decision, etc. It must be a relief and exciting at the same time. Sometimes though, we get drawn into a huge goal and don't ever sit back to ask the important question: why?

Why as in, what is your goal and vision for your college experience? Are you there because this is the next logical step to becoming a scientist, engineer, or a lawyer? Are you there because this is what everyone else is doing? Are you there because this is what your parents want? This needs to be brought into focus.

I am not bringing this up because I am advocating that you should just opt out of college because you don't feel like it or aren't sure what your major or career is. Also, some things like parental pressure can be good since your parents have a wealth of experience and knowledge about the real world they may typically advise you about. However, once you step on campus it is up to you to be successful, and if you do not know yourself and your goals then you're likely going to be mediocre at best or doomed at worst. The full decision on whether to go to college versus a trade school or entrepreneurship and which college to choose is beyond the scope of this book. What is most important is that you know why you're going to college and how to make the best of it.

Again, I want to emphasize I am not claiming you have to know exactly who you want to be in life, but by having a vision to succeed you can ensure you will be *somebody* rather than endlessly drifting to "find yourself." Self-discovery is an important part of college, but it should be part of your journey and not some ephemeral final destination. Most of us are still finding ourselves into old age, so four years wasted on only this vain pursuit to the detriment of solid performance is not a good strategy.

Write down your goals

Often, the best way to clarify one's thoughts is to write them down, which is what I suggest. In fact, if you're a fan of journals, starting a new one for college can be a great way to later self-reflect and keep track of your progress and changes. However, at a minimum I suggest before reading the rest of this book, you start a journal and write on the first page, *My Purpose for My College Experience*. Over several pages, you will be able to write down your general idea of college and major expectations, measurable goals, and any fears you may have.

First up is a section that you can call *General Expectations*, or something similar. Write down, preferably on one page, what you plan to get out of college. For example, you may want to "have a good time," "make lifelong friends," and "get into a good law school." This doesn't have to include everything you plan to do in college, and it may not even call out a specific career or major. It can even be a bit cheeky and aspirational such as "I want to become more personable" or even "meet some great women." These are all important parts of college and something you should look forward to doing. The purpose of this section is to lay out your general expectations and clear goals by which you can measure your accomplishments.

Though academics are the main reason you're in college—and this book will stress that to a fault—the college experience is indeed a waste if you become an introvert, only good at reading for classes and doing homework problem sets.

This first section is where you try to understand all of your preconceptions about college and what you will experience there. Maybe you have been watching college themed movies like *Stomp the Yard* or old-school ones such as *Animal House* or *School Daze* and have certain expectations of what you want college to be like. Even if these are the wrong expectations, it is best to be truthful upfront so you can analyze them later.

The next section is for your measurable goals. Measurable goals are more concrete such as a grade point average (GPA) goal, a goal to get into a certain graduate school, or a plan on how to pay for your education. These are goals which are relatively easy to track your progress against. For those who want to be engineers, doctors, or lawyers this could be easy. For example, if you're going to medical school, you need to know upfront what will be required. What GPA or Medical College Admission Test (MCAT) score will you need in order to get into your preferred medical school? What classes do you need to take? All of this, at least paraphrased, should be put down as measurable goals.

For those without such rigorously defined career paths, there are still definitely certain goals you can write down. Though it may seem funny, one goal many people can put down is to "finish in four (or five) years." Some people drop out and others seem to want to drag out college for six years and beyond at great expense.

Next, you can look at other achievements. At the very least you can say something like "graduate with honors."

Yes, these goals may change over time and you may look back at sometime in the future and see these as being trite or even misguided. However, they'll help focus you, and even if you have to change course, like many will during college, if you have at least some basic self-direction it will help you make the right decision and not waste time drifting aimlessly.

Letter to yourself

Another effective way to keep track of your goals is write a letter to yourself describing your current situation and your expectations for the semester or year. This can be in part of your journal or on a piece of paper sealed in an envelope. Put it in a safe place and read it when the semester or year ends. This can help you compare your current life, which has likely changed in a lot of unpredictable ways, with your past expectations. Reading this letter can help you see how you have changed and whether your goals have changed for the better or gone off-track. It can also be funny to see how much we can mature, even in only four months.

Be yourself

As the final section of this chapter, it is important to emphasize that college will change you but that you should always be yourself. I remember when I went to college I thought I was going to dump everything I had been in high school and change into some new smooth persona like Eddie Murphy in *The Nutty Professor*. It didn't happen, and in retrospect I am happy I kept an even keel.

Lots of people go to college and try to create an alternate self that they think their peers or the world will value more. They may go from being the quiet kid in high school to trying to become a big-time player or try to downplay their middle-class or affluent origins and act like a thug in a bizarre quest to seem real. I have known guys whose parents drive $50,000 cars and have three-thousand-plus square-foot homes only to see their sons try to turn gangsta. It is pretty pitiful, and the sad part is these people can typically be called out, especially by those who grew up in less privileged situations and realize that lifestyle is far from the glory and bling of rap videos. Some people buy into their act though so it continues.

I will repeat the immortal words of Chuck D from Public Enemy who spoke on my campus about a similar topic: don't be a college thug. The two are almost contradictions. That does not mean I'm against people being manly and that I want everyone to act like soft "beta" males, far from it. You should not have to check your manhood at the door in college. The worst part about being a thug is it perpetuates the worst stereotypes about Blacks, often to other students who have little experience with Blacks. It often degrades academic achievement in order to look cool. Most thugs don't like to say they can't hang out because it's time to study. Not being a thug doesn't preclude you from wearing your favorite brand of urban gear, listening to the best hip hop, or even using vernacular in casual conversation. If you came from a less-privileged background, not being thug also doesn't mean you have to be ashamed of where you came from. It just means you don't project a bogus attitude of some foolish notion of street cred. People with real street smarts can exude it naturally, without the buffoonery.

In conclusion, the over 2,000 year old quote from Sun Tzu in *The Art of War* with which I opened the chapter still stands. In order to hope for college success you must know yourself and know the enemy, which in this case is college. Understanding and succeeding in college will occupy the remainder of the book and with the knowledge of both, your success is ensured.

Chapter 2
Academics

Education is the passport to the future, for tomorrow belongs to those who prepare for it today.
—Malcolm X

Too often the educational value of doing well what is done, however little, is overlooked. One thing well done prepares the mind to do the next thing better. Not how much, but how well, should be the motto. One problem thoroughly understood is of more value than a score poorly mastered...show me a youth that is dabbling in all subjects and mastering none, and I will show you a man that will go floundering through life without purpose, without business, without stability, without top or bottom.
—Booker T. Washington

When you control a man's thinking you do not have to worry about his actions. You do not have to tell him not to stand here or go yonder. He will find his 'proper place' and will stay in it. You do not need to send him to the back door. He will go without being told. In fact, if there is no back door, he will cut one for his special benefit. His education makes it necessary.
—Carter G. Woodson, The Mis-Education of the Negro

Let us start this chapter out clearly. The academic work of college is, by and large, the overarching reason why you are attending, and the majority of your efforts must be directed accordingly. If this is at all controversial to you then I would say you are not fully prepared for college and need to clarify your values. Yes, there are other important life lessons such as making lifelong friends and networking, but are you paying $35,000+ a year to socialize?

All other activities you undertake in college should either help you achieve academic success at best or not detract from academic success at worst. Unless you're on an athletic scholarship or have to work full-time to pay your way through school, I have yet to see a convincing argument why you should take on any activities in college that will severely damage you academically. Even with those two exceptions there are ways to keep caught up and minimize the harm to your grades. Again, if you disagree with this, why are you paying thousands of dollars for something you could use more wisely elsewhere?

The difference between learning, education, and being educated

There are several ways one can receive knowledge, both through your own efforts or having knowledge imparted to you. However, not all of these are the same and going to college requires a clear distinction of each. Learning happens whenever you encounter new knowledge or an experience that you end up using to change your thoughts, actions, and behavior. Learning has been happening in and out of the classroom since you were born. Learning is also something that you don't need college for since a lot of it can be had for free from the Internet or the local public library. You are in college to learn, but more than just what you get in the classroom. Otherwise, what would distinguish one college from another besides the size of the library and quality of the class syllabi?

Education is what most people are looking to further in college. It involves a lot more than just learning raw facts but learning about different philosophies and outlooks, analyzing the world as a whole, and becoming prepared to be an active participant in it. The first thing you must learn is whether you go to the local community college or Harvard, your education is first and foremost your responsibility. The second thing is that your education must come from outside the classroom as much or more than from inside it. Finally, you cannot go to college naively wanting to be "filled" with knowledge and blindly accepting whatever you are given as holy writ. You must learn to critically analyze both your own ideas as well as those from a professor.

This final point brings us to the difference between getting an education and being educated. There are a lot of very intelligent people who go to college and do well in their course work only to come out with little more knowledge of how the world works than when they came in. Worse, they may think they have knowledge and not question the basic assumptions behind the world view that they were taught and therefore can become arrogant or self-confident about the actual state of their learning.

I studied business as an undergrad, and we were often taught about advanced financial concepts and stock market trends as if they were a given. For those who went into finance, the last several years have provided a rude awakening on how valid these concepts really were.

You must get an education and not let anyone else tell you what to be or make you into an assembly line product. This is very much a danger since higher education is a business like any other and like most businesses, what universities are marketing about themselves to students is often different than what they signal to employers. For employers they often signal you can be satisfied that our students will be of a certain standard. In order to achieve this, there is some need to homogenize the output and this is done throughout college by shared rituals, institutions, academic core courses, and career guidance. The big investment banks hire at Wharton and the University of Chicago, not because they think this is the only way to find smart people—it isn't—but that they know they're getting someone with a predetermined outlook molded by both personal and academic factors and that they are trained in certain ways.

Economists actually study this phenomenon by research into the "signaling" effects that diplomas from higher education provide. To a certain extent, the university views you as a product, and don't forget this. This does not mean they are completely crass and uncaring, it just means you can't expect your heart's desire to be handed to you on a silver platter.

You'll only get out of college what you want to get out of it, and if you aren't getting what you want in the standard curriculum, there are guerrilla methods for furthering your education. Some of these will be discussed as we go through this section. There are some books you should think about reading to get education in perspective before you go to college or while you are there. A great start is *The Mis-Education of the Negro* by Carter G. Woodson, which is a classic on how to be badly educated. Booker T. Washington's *Up from Slavery* and W.E.B. DuBois's *The Souls of Black Folks* also present good views of how to view education and what is most important, though the two don't always agree on the latter point. A great essay is also given by Marcus Garvey (and as of print was available on the webpage of the University of California, Los Angeles Marcus Garvey Papers site).

Titled "Intelligence, Education, Universal Knowledge and How to Get It," it also discusses the importance of education and how to educate yourself. Of course Sun Tzu's *The Art of War*, which I quoted in the first chapter is a must read as its lessons apply well to life. Benjamin Franklin's *Poor Richard's Almanac* and *The Way to Wealth* are short but detailed sources for important advice on living successfully as are many quotes from Thomas Jefferson on the topic of education, though they are diffused throughout a variety of sources. Finally, a somewhat subversive and provocative look at the priorities and purposes of higher education is provided by Jeff Schmidt in his interesting book, *Disciplined Minds*. You may not have the time to read most of these but they can provide a great service in helping you use college to further your own educational goals.

Libraries

Throughout history, libraries have shone as beacons of knowledge. There were libraries of clay cuneiform tablets in ancient Sumer, libraries in Ancient Egypt culminating with the great library of Alexandria, and so on. With the advent of the printing press in China and then Europe, libraries became much more common as books became cheaper and easier to mass produce.

The first universities were often just a bunch of scholars and a library. Today's modern universities often have libraries that may contain more books than had ever been written five hundred years ago. Knowledge of the library and its workings are essential to your academic career and is part of the reason I mention them first.

I once knew a guy in college who bragged about not having to go into the library at all for two years. His grades were ok as far as I knew, but there is something unnerving about being alright with this kind of ignorance. If you just want to get by and "be educated," then maybe this will work, but if you want to get an education, you need to understand the library's ins and outs.

Most universities have multiple libraries—a large one dedicated to the liberal arts with smaller ones dedicated to different fields such as engineering, physics, art, or music. Usually the larger library will have a tour at the beginning of each semester for new students to familiarize them with its layout and resources. I encourage you to take it. This will save you time later when you have the daunting task of doing a research project.

Libraries typically have two major classes of resources: books and journals/databases. Books are kept in "the stacks," which are multi-floor massive collections. These are organized by Dewey decimal numbers, the library book classification system, and their corresponding subjects. Unlike when I was in school and card catalogs were just heading out the door to be replaced by computers, everything is now online and finding call numbers for books should be easy. Searching the stacks can be quick and painless once you know how to do it well.

Journals/databases are now mostly online, but you will still need to know what's out there and which resources are best for different types of searches. ISI Web of Science helps you search for scientific papers while Lexis-Nexis is better suited for searches on legal issues. You'll need to find out which databases are available and know when to use them. Since most of these are now online you can often surf them from the comfort of your dorm room or your preferred Wi-Fi location, however, some older archives may still be in print format and require a visit to the stacks.

One of the things you need to know is how to check out books and the restrictions placed on checkouts. Normal books can sometimes be yours for up to a semester unless another student submits a recall that forces you to turn it in sooner. Others, on reserve by professors, can only be checked out for a few hours. You must always keep track of library books and return them on time. College books are often expensive and out-of-print, which can mean horrendous replacement costs. Fines that you do not pay can also keep you from graduating! Also, this goes without saying, but never intentionally damage a book or journal. This has been the practice in the past (before journals were online) when people would rip out important pages or articles to give them an edge against other students. This is completely unacceptable and could lead to severe disciplinary consequences from the university.

Libraries are also great places to study. They provide quiet and spacious areas with power plugs and usually omnipresent Wi-Fi. The larger libraries are often open until midnight or later and sometimes 24-7 during final exams. It may be useful to find a nice corner to study in the library for yourself or a group. If the main libraries are too crowded sometimes other libraries, like physics or music, have good hours but are not as busy and can provide a less distracting study environment.

Academic course load

One of the main determinants of your academic success will be the selection of your academic classes. In general there are several reasons to choose a class:

1. It's a required core course that all students need to complete.

2. The course is required by your major/minor. These include lower-level courses you have to take to get to interesting higher level courses.

3. You are required by a graduate school such as medical school to take the class.

4. It's something you take out of self-interest or career aspirations.

5. You want to shore up your GPA.

6. The class balances out your schedule.

You must choose your classes in a manner that is conducive to your college goals but also that allows you to pursue your own interests and broaden your horizons. In accordance with this, for popular classes or specific professors you may have to plan your main classes up to a year in advance. For example, if you need to take CHEM 201 for medical school but you want to take a history class in the same time slot, and it's only once a year, you should plan to take the required class first and make sure you register early to get the history class the following year. Or if you couldn't get into a class with a great professor, you have to weigh the pros and cons of waiting for another semester when this class is available versus taking the same class with a less exciting professor. If you're going to put off a relatively specialized class, often you may want to email the professor to make sure it will be taught the next year. Sometimes professors go on sabbaticals, which are one or more years where they take off from teaching to do research. In those cases you may only have one chance to take a class before you graduate.

In addition, you must keep track of the number of credits you earn and necessary core classes to ensure on-time graduation. If you do this correctly, you'll be able to balance out your course load throughout your college career and perhaps even be able to take a light or easy course load your final semester before graduation. It's inexcusable to "miss" taking a class and being stuck in a rush to finish it before graduation or having to delay graduation. Also, if you balance your course load you can spread out more difficult classes to ensure you will not be overwhelmed. For example, if you are not the best in math and science, taking calculus, organic chemistry, and physics in one semester is a recipe for stress and perhaps poor performance in all three. This is another reason to be proactive in scheduling classes. If you know what you need to take for your major, you should look ahead at least a semester, preferably a year, to make sure you can balance your course load and get the best professors for each class.

Sometimes you may have to have all of your courses done by the end of your junior year. For example, if you are applying to medical school in the first semester of your senior year, you want to make sure you get everything done by your junior year.

Once you know the classes you need or want to take, you can look at how to schedule them. There are several things to keep in mind. For example, many classes have teacher assistant (TA) sessions taught by upperclassmen or graduate students. Other classes have labs. Sometimes the TA sessions are optional and people decide they can schedule another regular class in that time period. This is a bad idea. TA sessions are important, especially since they give help on the homework and TAs have often seen the exams in advance. They may give extra help to students who attend their sessions by giving problem examples very similar to test material. You could be at a serious disadvantage if you decide not to attend these.

Labs are usually held once or twice a week for several hours in the afternoon or evening, and are for experiments or other hands-on work to emphasize the theory learned in class. Since these are usually mandatory you can't schedule over or skip them. It may be an error, however, to load up on classes with labs so that you have one almost every day. This can take valuable time and the post-lab work such as notebooks or lab write-ups can be laborious in addition to your standard homework. For labs make sure you are familiar with all lab directions as well as safety around various reagents and organisms. If you are in a lab group, make sure the group fairly distributes work so that no one person is burdened with write-ups and gets all the benefit of the work.

There are other things to think about in choosing and scheduling classes. For example, you need to eat lunch (more about this in the health chapter). If you are in class from 10:00 A.M. until noon and then 1:00 P.M. until 3:00 P.M., you may realize you won't have time to grab lunch if you're in a class far from a cafeteria or eatery since you have to factor in getting to your next class on time.

Also, don't run away from a class just because it's early. Sometimes the best way to structure your day is to wake up early and get your classes done as soon as possible. Sleeping in until ten or eleven every day may seem fun, but it's not an enviable sleep pattern (more on this in health as well).

Despite saying all this, however, getting the perfect schedule is not always easy and you may have to make frequent adjustments at the beginning of the semester. This brings us to the subject of add/drop deadlines and waitlists. The add period is where you can get into a class without special permission and problems with paperwork. The drop period is when you can get out of a class without any record you were ever in it. You need to be vigilant about the add/drop deadlines for classes and act as soon as possible to make changes. The add period deadline is important to make since if you're not signing up for classes early, your preferred classes and timeslots may fill up. If you want to get into a class, you have to figure it out by this time. Also, the drop period deadline is important since it is the last day you can drop a class without it being on your transcript as incomplete. You need to figure out if you want to take a class as quickly as possible. Typically, you should always have a backup class(es) in case you don't get into the one you want or find a class you're in isn't necessary or not something you want to bother with. Again, the key is planning.

Often a great class or a necessary class is full and you can't add it with the normal procedures. This is when you often have to go on the waitlist. It's important you arrange this with the professor, TA, or registrar immediately after the class meets for the first time. Also, if this class is really a big deal, keep the space open in your schedule so if you get in you won't have conflicts. Check by the professor's office during office hours to see how the waitlist is going and if it looks impossible, get into one of your backup plan classes. Email the professor thanking him or her for the opportunity and asking if there is a way you can arrange to be at the front of the line for the next time the class is offered. It may not work, but it can't hurt.

Some classes are known by various names such as *easy*, *gut*, or something similar because they have a reputation for having a low workload and an easy grade. These classes are usually filled for the obvious reasons. Gut classes can be acceptable as ways to boost your GPA or take an interesting topic with little stress. However, they should not be used to avoid work elsewhere. Also, some professors, when they get wind that their class is considered an easy A, tighten the screws and shock a few people to keep everyone on their toes. The moral of the story is never approach a class with an attitude that this is an A with no effort. If the plan was to boost your GPA, you will be shocked if you land a C!

Remedial classes

Sometimes you'll take a placement test and your scores on some or all sections will dictate you should be doing remedial work. Whatever else you may think and however many of your friends are in remedial class with you, treat this as a crisis do-or-die situation. By taking time to do remedial courses, you're already behind most of the student population and will struggle to get to the same footing. For this reason these classes should receive your utmost attention and study.

Remedial classes can sometimes carry a stigma of inferiority that can affect the performance of people in them. The thing to remember is being in a remedial class does not make you a failure. Not everyone has the same educational opportunities and what kept you in good stead in high school may not prepare you for what's to come in college. On the other hand, flunking a remedial class does mean you aren't a fit for whatever college you happen to be in, which is why hardcore studying is critical.

Choosing a major and a minor

This is a very personal topic for a variety of reasons because it can be very formative in determining your career, at least your first job, and grad school possibilities. Your major can be a combination of what you want to do for a living, what you like, and what you feel your strengths are. If you want to be an engineer or a scientist, your major is pretty much clear. However, if you want to go to medical school, law school, become a teacher, or are considering grad school, in a general sense the majors can be more open to personal preference and aspiration. The breakout of majors for Black Americans according to the Department of Education is shown in Figure 4 as a reference of what people generally major in (not necessarily what you should do).

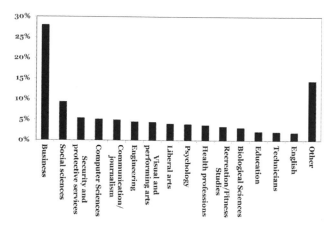

FIGURE 4—Breakdown of majors for Black Americans

So how to choose a major? First, find out what the major really means, not what you think it means. Read the class descriptions of the major to see what the classes entail. Talk to upperclassmen in that major about their experience. Also, to see career path viability, talk to someone high up in the department or the career center about what the typical career trajectory and employment has been for graduates in that major. Internet research can also help to see what academic or professional associations for this major exist and can also help you see what opportunities it can hold for you.

As much as college can be about self-fulfillment, its freedom can be a rope to pull yourself up or to hang yourself. The stark reality is that certain majors are more marketable than others, especially in the hard economic times we currently experience. A major can mean the difference between looking for jobs months after graduation and having a job upon graduation. A lot of people, even some faculty, will tell you not to worry about the jobs since college is more than job training and you need a well-rounded education. I agree, but I am also realistic. In an age when college fees are skyrocketing and the supply of new jobs for graduates is shrinking, you need to realize that your loans will come due and you may need to support yourself right after graduation. Therefore, choosing a marketable major is not a wrong decision if you have no clear postgraduate pursuits for a masters or PhD.

I don't want to ruffle feathers but the job market has often sent clear signals that in hard times it wants people with marketable skills. This often tends to be science and engineering, business, economics, political science, and sometimes psychology or foreign languages.

I loved the classes I took in history, English, and philosophy and heard good things about others such as African-American studies, sociology, or various other niche liberal arts majors. However, it can put you at a serious disadvantage in the job market. Employers are often open to students of any major but when times are tight, they look for the most skills and people who need the least amount of training. I didn't create this world, I just explain what I've seen.

Oftentimes, a good compromise can be choosing a major that is very marketable and choosing a double major or minor in a subject you enjoy. This is a way of hedging your bets and allowing you to make sure you may have a marketable major and can take classes you enjoy. This was part of my own rationale for getting a BS in business and completing the requirements for a BA in physics.

You want to think carefully about your major since it is a significant disruption of your graduation schedule if you have to change midstream. If you do have to change majors, take a hard look at why. Is it because of difficulty? If so, ask yourself if you're throwing in the towel too early and if you can possibly get more help such as extra tutoring. If you need to change majors, carefully work out how it will affect the number of credits you need to graduate and the financial cost to you and your parents if you need to stay for extra semesters. The cost may be worth it if you find a major is totally unsuitable for you but discovering this earlier rather than later can make the transition more seamless. There is nothing shameful in changing your major for the right reasons. Many times people find they are out of their depth in engineering or hate the advanced courses in sociology, however, if you do good research on your major early, you may be able to save yourself from a radical re-orientation in your sophomore or junior year.

A minor is a degree that requires completing fewer courses in a discipline than a major. These can be alternatives to a double major and also allow you to receive formal credit for a topic you have an interest in but for which don't want to or cannot pursue a full major.

Buying books

Of all the expenses you (or your parents) calculated when you figured out how much to budget for school, the cost of books is one often overlooked. Books can put you out of $1,000 to $2,000 a semester, so it's hardly a trivial amount. Regardless of what school you go to, chances are the school bookstore is the most expensive, albeit convenient, way you can shop. What usually happens is people don't think about getting books until the day before class and the school bookstore is the path of least resistance. Often the problem is the syllabus is not distributed until the first day of class, allowing less time to prepare to search for alternate sources for textbooks, though this is less of a problem now with the Internet.

One of the first questions people have when confronted with these costs is if they really have to buy all of the books. Typically yes, but not always. With large textbooks and packets of articles, you usually need a copy. People can share to save money but then it can cause friction if someone wants to hog it during exam time. For classes that require a lot of reading of books or novels, you may get away with borrowing the books from friends or the library if you prepare early enough. You have to use your judgment.

One of the ways to cut costs is to look online. Amazon is a common choice, but Alibris can also have used copies for much cheaper. The biggest obstacle to this method of saving money by getting used textbooks is the textbook edition. Publishers are not stupid and realize that to maximize revenue and profit, they need to reduce the viability of the aftermarket for used books. Therefore they release a new edition every year or two with additional content and new (or rearranged) chapter exercises to force you to buy a new book. If a professor specifies a certain edition, you usually need to get it. The material is often not drastically different but end-of-chapter problems may be. Another option that has just become possible in the last couple of years is to purchase an ebook copy of a textbook, which is often cheaper. This will require you to have an e-reader and be comfortable with using it though (see the chapter on technology).

Many people have tried copying textbooks. Just so you know, this is illegal due to copyright laws though it isn't common that people get turned in for it. It is not too convenient though since at ten cents a page, a 300-page textbook would cost about $30 to copy, plus the couple of hours you have to stand there while it's copied. People have also bought foreign versions of textbooks from countries like India where the textbook is in English but at a much reduced price (and often the book is bound with inferior material and printed on lower quality paper). This is not illegal as long as you do not resell the book outside of India, which becomes copyright infringement.

The final and probably most common way to save money on books is to buy them used from those who have taken the class. They may still be expensive but paying $60 is better than paying $120. You may want to arrange this as early as possible since used copies tend to sell quickly and the price obviously goes up as the supply is constrained.

There are other school supplies that are essential. These include spiral-bound notebooks with dividers and paper, which are good for notes and handouts. Don't forget to put your name and email in your binders and organizers in case you leave them somewhere. Other good supplies to get, preferably off-campus where they are cheaper, are printer paper, printer ink or toner, plenty of pencils and pens, correction tape, and a sturdy backpack. With the advent of tablet computers like iPads, paper notebooks may be obsolete, but I am still a fan of the old pencil and paper. Your paper notebook doesn't crash and no one wants to steal it.

Going to class

So classes are starting. And you need to be there...on time! Going to class sounds so elementary you may wonder why it has its own section. I will just state common sense is not so common and it cannot hurt to repeat the obvious. First and foremost, if you sign up for a class, go to it. No excuses. If it is at 8:00 A.M., then you need to get to bed by 1:00 A.M. to get the at least the six hours of sleep most people need. Of course going to bed earlier is better. The best way to go to class is to develop a routine. Wake up and maybe work out and then get breakfast and head to class. Your deadline for arrival should be five minutes before it starts. Professors typically start on time and you need time to find a seat, especially if you want to be inconspicuous.

Make sure you dress presentably. Though schools are much more casual than in the days when colleges made you dress up to go to class, it pays to be presentable. If you know you have trouble getting up, shave, pack your bag, and put out your clothes out the night before. In the morning, the less you have to think about, the better.

Once you arrive in class, sit somewhere where you can clearly see the professor and any material presented and away from anyone who will be disruptive or distracting. As an exception, I am all for sitting next to cute girls, but just don't talk during class. The professor and the class should receive your full attention. Your cell phone should be on silent and you should not check calls or texts during class. If you can bring coffee or energy drinks to stay awake, do so. You don't want to be the sleepyhead called out during class in front of everyone.

The overall plan of a class is listed on the syllabus, which most people don't read. The syllabus is important because it outlines the professor's expectations, the class textbooks, and the breakdown of the overall grade between papers and exams. I had one professor who stated on his syllabus that he would give five extra points to the first twenty people who notified him they'd read the syllabus. Surprisingly, a lot of people missed this freebie, which emphasized the point that most people don't read the syllabus.

The grading information is likely the most crucial. If your midterm is fifty percent of your grade and your homework ten percent, it tells you that you better know your stuff by the midterm though you have more leeway in the homework assignments. If it is the opposite, you better concentrate on the homework and maybe get a study group.

Classes are typically either in large lecture halls or small classrooms depending on the class size. In a small class, you better not be late, and you better participate since you will easily stick out if you don't. In a larger lecture hall it is easier to be anonymous but don't be the person who always comes in late or you won't be anonymous. Some large lectures don't allow many questions because of the number of students, so it's often best to sit in a seat where you see all the action well during the lecture.

Class participation can be important and may be part of your grade. When you need to participate, it's crucial that you read and understand the assigned material. Many professors can smell a BS line pretty easily and respond accordingly. Sometimes I wrote down some key questions to ask in my notebook before I got to class to make sure I could attempt to sound intelligent and show I read the material. Also, if asked a question by the professor, give as good an answer as you can but don't be afraid to say you don't know if you don't have a clue.

As stated before, you should attend the TA sessions and TA office hours. Even then, you should attend around exam time since often hints on exam material can be given out. Being on the TA's good side never hurts since he or she often grades the exams for the professors. Many TAs have office hours and attending those can help you get additional help and form rapport with them. You should definitely attend professor office hours, if only to discuss the class and gain rapport. If you are a real name to him or her and not a number, you never know how it can help you in the final grading.

How to study

If you are just skimming this book, fine but if you have to read a section thoroughly, make it this one. This is one of the skills that will make or break you in college. I saw so many people drop out or have to cancel their dreams due in large part to poor study habits than almost any other cause. This should be the first skill you master if you want to succeed in college. It is something you must seek out for yourself because no one can put a gun to your head and tell you how to "study hard." From the outset I will state something that may shock people. The study habits you had in high school of just going home and doing homework are likely very inadequate for the rigors of college.

Let me tell you the story of a typical freshman, Derrick. Derrick was an ace at his high school. He did well in his classes and was admired by his teachers and peers. His good 3.8-plus grades and SAT scores earned him a place at a prestigious college. He was all set—until he got his midterm grades first semester. Derrick had never gotten a C in his life, but here he had several. He had noticed in class he felt a bit less prepared than other students but had shrugged it off as due to his own lack of confidence. A 2.5 interim GPA is a real shock but that's what he got. He wonders where he went wrong. Is he really cut out to be an engineer?

This story has happened thousands of times. One of the first things you realize in college is that it probably doesn't matter that you were hot stuff in high school. Here there are people who are blazing fireballs, geniuses of the like you have never seen. They have gone to elite public or private schools and have been honed in the study habits that college would demand. You may struggle to keep pace.

So how do you prevent this from happening? What can you do to buckle down and make sure the first semester is a resounding success? I have a concept I've thought about called EdCon. Those who are familiar with defense conditions probably also see the similarity. DefCon (defense condition) was invented by the United States government during the Cold War to define the current state of military preparedness. DefCon 5 was peace with little or no threats. DefCon 1 was the onset of nuclear war.

Similarly, EdCon defines how hard you should be studying given the conditions. The EdCon conditions defined below will be used throughout the book to help you gauge whether you're being serious enough for what college requires:

> EdCon 5—Typically summer and winter vacation or post-exam periods. There is work to be done such as reading ahead.

> EdCon 4—Basic nightly studying, mostly light reading as needed to keep up in classes,

nothing stressful. Usually only applies the first week or two of the semester.

EdCon 3—Substantial homework and reading is required to keep up in class. You need to budget several hours nightly to do what is required as well as some reading ahead.

EdCon 2—Hardcore studying is required in order to prepare for an upcoming exam, paper, or presentation. You need to structure your days and weekends to accommodate the amount of work. This includes cutting down on partying, seeing your boo, and hanging with the boys. All nighters are possible.

EdCon 1—You are in deep crap. This is likely because you're failing, will fail, or will be kicked out of school without a drastic improvement in grades. This requires drastic action for the entire semester including almost no socializing during the week, minimal socialization (i.e. one party) on the weekends, and the removal of all unnecessary distractions apart from work or scholarship athletics. If you aren't serious now you'll join the ranks of college dropouts later. One or more all nighters may be necessary.

The typical state during the semester is usually EdCon 3 dropping to EdCon 2 around midterms and finals. EdCon 1 is never a situation you want to confront unless you're starting out with remedial classes. If you're doing EdCon 4 all semester, you're not taking the right course load. If you're doing EdCon 5 at all during school you're seriously screwing up and will soon be doing EdCon 1.

So how do you adapt to the EdCon levels? The first thing you have to state with absolute confidence is *I and I alone am responsible for maintaining the appropriate study habits for school.* It's not up to your boys, the girl(s) you are dating or sleeping with, your professors, your parents, God, the mailman, Rick Ross, or anyone else. If you don't man up, you're through. There are certain techniques to master to study appropriately, which we will elaborate on below.

Study environment

The first thing you have to control is your study environment. This is the place you study. The area should have several key features: a minimum amount of distraction, enough space to spread out your books and notebooks to do work, easy access to restrooms or food and drinks, and accessibility at most hours of the day. This can be your dorm room, but this is often difficult because of the distractions from dorm mates or computers. A typical choice is the library, either in a study room or the stacks. In order to minimize distractions you should let people know when you're studying, you're really studying. That means answering texts with "Ltr man, I have to do this work" or just not answering at all.

The perfect study environment will allow complete concentration on the task at hand for hours at a time. It is okay to take a break every hour or so to stretch, grab some coffee, or even make a call.

However, keep your breaks to fifteen minutes max to avoid ruining your rhythm.

The location is usually a personal preference. If you are tight on cash, it's best to avoid studying in coffee shops or cafeterias where you will feel compelled to spend money. Bringing your favorite drink and finding a quiet place on campus should work.

When to study

Again, this depends on your classes and extracurriculars, but this must be a scheduled time every day. The best times are typically multiple-hour gaps between classes when you have at least an hour available, though taking any time to read or work on problems is a smart strategy. Always remember fatigue and hunger inhibit your ability to focus, so the best time to get work done is when you're not too tired or hungry to focus properly. Granted during some periods of the semester, it's impossible to not be extremely fatigued all the time.

You should structure study time so you don't have to study too late into the night since you want to keep a reasonable sleep schedule to be functional in class each day. Whether your stop time is 9:00 P.M. or midnight is up to you. You need to avoid scheduling too many extracurricular or social activities that eat into study time. If you have one night a week you're really busy that's fine, but you need to prepare accordingly. You can spread out your study time if you have days such as Tuesdays/Thursdays where you have fewer classes.

Studying on the weekend can be difficult for many people. Partying all night and sleeping with a possible hangover the next morning can eat into weekend study time. Most people only study Sunday night, but this is a mistake. A better strategy is to study a few hours in the afternoon on Saturday, or all day in an EdCon 2 or 1 situation, to avoid cramming all your week's work on one day. Granted with sporting events and other activities, weekends can get packed, but there are usually a few hours you can schedule. You should typically keep the Friday and Saturday evenings open obviously since the parties, socializing, and dating often are best during these times.

During exam periods after the end of the regular semester, you need to be typically in EdCon 2 mode except the first Friday night when everyone parties. Just because you have no classes doesn't mean this is a social hour. You need to sprint to the end just like a race.

Preparation

When we first told the story of Derrick, we talked about how his high school habits were not adequate. Why? What is wrong with just going home and doing homework and going to class? In college, there are several other things you must do to be successful.

First, you should be outlining and reading ahead. At any given point in the school year you need to be at least *two classes ahead* in your reading in order to keep pace. Yes, you should read ahead to keep pace since difficult material can often put you behind if you just read according to the class schedule. If you are really on top of things, you should also have done the homework assignments for those two classes as well. As I will discuss later, people serious about engineering and pre-med should read the textbooks of the most difficult subjects before the semester begins! Yes, I said before the semester. That way, throughout the semester it is all review, and whatever misunderstandings you have can be cleared up without the struggle of learning new and hard material.

Also, when I mean read, I don't just mean scan the text. You need to learn how to outline and outline the text as you go. Writing ensures a greater retention and comprehension than just reading and the notes from your outlines and the class can be invaluable study aids come exam time. For those who are wondering, this is typical EdCon 3 work and not even considered cramming.

Of course any memorization flash cards or problem sets for that future material are also necessary. I don't mean to scare anyone but as I stated in the first chapter, if your objective is to succeed and educate yourself, you'll do what's necessary. Trust me, once you find out how to do this well, it will hardly crowd out all the time for having fun and going out. It will make having fun a lot less stressful though since you aren't in EdCon 1.

Keep copies of graded homework assignments and answers so you can remember your mistakes and not repeat them on exams. Around exam time a helpful resource can be old exams, but make sure these are from approved sources (i.e., The professor) and not the gray market variety that students have kept and are distributed without permission. In some places having the latter can be considered cheating.

When you fall into an EdCon 2 or 1 situation, which will inevitably happen at least once, you need to know the pros and cons of cramming, which, in general, is not an effective way to study. Cramming will happen, but if you expect it to change your fate if you have been at EdCon 5 or 4 all semester you are sadly mistaken. Sometimes this can lead to the feared all-nighter where you end up working from dusk till dawn, showering, and then going straight to class. This is not a failure, but it's best to manage your time to prevent it as much as you can and not make it a way of life. In general, for an exam you should ramp up studying a week ahead of time, covering all necessary material. On the day before the exam, it's best to stop in the late afternoon and relax as much as you can. Go out to eat, go on a date, see a movie, or just play video games. This will help your mind relax and remember, the knowledge you have stored isn't going anywhere.

Study groups and tutoring

Study groups are an important part of any study regimen, particularly in math, science, and engineering. They may be informal or set up by the class. It's best to get involved with a study group early since it's a great way to meet people and work on homework and studying with usually beneficial results. Don't fall prey to the false pride that you can only study by yourself. If you ever tire of a study group you can drop out, but joining later in the semester may not be as easy, and if you're behind the group may see you as more of a liability than a benefit.

Study groups can meet in the library, where there are often special rooms, and this allows the most focus and least distraction. Meeting in dorm rooms or suites can work too, but I've often seen this break down into socializing. You need at least one person in the group whose job it is to keep everybody on task and make sure things get done. This person doesn't have to be a study nazi but just a regulator of sorts.

Tutoring is a subject near and dear to my heart. I still to this day don't understand why more people don't seek out help earlier, especially for the free services offered by the school or departments. Here's my advice: the first time you get a bad grade on homework or a quiz, get a tutor or at least go to the TA's office hours. Don't wait until the midterm or God forbid the final to think someone can teach you what you need to know. This will likely not happen, regardless of the tutor's talent or your dedication. Tutoring is the equivalent of taking swimming lessons—it's not a life preserver that can be thrown out when you've already fallen off the boat.

Often, the school may have opportunities for free or cheap tutoring, which can be available at various costs from other undergraduate or graduate students. You still have to take the initiative to get it when you need it though. At school I tutored computer science and physics for the Office of African-American Affairs. It was free for two hours once a week. The sad thing is, I think maybe thirty percent of the students who showed up were Black. This was probably not due to the relative proportions of Blacks in the student population. Often, only one student showed up or none. We had the professors advertise the service so I don't think people were unaware, and I knew people complained about how hard the class was in computer science (programming C++). I often had people call me right before finals though to try to learn everything. It never really worked out.

Academic dishonesty

There are few things you can do at school that can damage your reputation for life besides academic dishonesty. The stench of it will pollute your character for years and even decades. If you ever become someone important, you'll probably live in fear of someone finding out about your past malfeasance. To be honest, I'll even go as far as to say only getting arrested or getting a girl pregnant can derail your academic career as much as academic dishonesty.

The statistics about academic dishonesty are pretty depressing. A study by the Center for Academic Integrity in 2010 showed forty percent of student respondents admitted to copying a few sentences into written papers without attribution. People cheat and think nothing of it. Oftentimes these shining examples of "merit" cheated through high school, had people ghostwrite or at least help them write college essays, and got away with it. So why would they stop in college? If you have ever engaged in this type of behavior, stop now. If you haven't, don't ever think it's okay because the masses engage in it. If you're caught, you have no excuse and you know Black men don't often get second chances.

There are several kinds of academic dishonesty I will profile here. The penalties of the different schools vary but usually the minimum is flunking the assignment, more often flunking the course, or in cases with cheating codes or honor systems, mandatory expulsion.

Cheating

I hope I don't have to explain to you what cheating is. It's a deliberate infraction of the rules of an assignment or test in the hope of an unfair advantage. This can mean smuggling in notes to tests (or writing notes on your hand), sneaking a peek at your neighbor's paper during a test, copying someone's homework assignment without actually doing the work, talking about test questions to someone who hasn't taken the exam yet, or even distributing copies of old tests that were supposed to be returned to the professor.

Don't do it. I know people will rationalize it saying most people don't get caught, but the ones who do pay a heavy price as an example. There's no reason to cheat. If you need help, we've already outlined other methods in this section. If you're going to get a bad grade, cheating isn't a way to stop it from happening.

If you're in a study group that has adopted cheating as an unspoken (or even spoken) ethic, leave it. If one of the members gets caught and squeals, it's like a murder case with accomplices but only one trigger man. You'll get thrown under the bus. If you're invited to cheat, decline. Whether or not to turn the person in is a personal decision and based on the school's ethic codes, but at the very least distance yourself from them in the academic context.

Plagiarism

Plagiarism is the use of the work of others as your own without giving credit or citation. This is a huge problem with papers. It's gotten even worse with the advent of the Internet where easy cut and paste allows you to look brilliant, though perhaps slightly incoherent, with a few key strokes. Plagiarism is more of an ego crime more often than cheating because you can usually put passages from the text you want in the text of papers as long as you cite them with footnotes or references. You should be very familiar with the MLA reference style and how to quote articles, books, or websites in a bibliography. If there's ever a doubt in your mind whether to cite something, cite it!

The flip side of computers and the Internet making plagiarism easier is that it makes it easier for you to get caught! There is now software to help professors find plagiarism in papers. One example was a professor at my alma mater, Louis Bloomfield, who taught a class on general physics called *How Things Work*. A large part of the grade was a term paper and being suspicious of plagiarism, he created a software program to compare text strings in papers across the years. What he found was massive cheating where people were using parts of papers from older years as their own. This ended up getting a lot of students expelled and revoking the degrees of some who had graduated! Professors often also type suspicious phrases into Google to see if they come up. If they find a phrase from your paper, you're in trouble.

Data Fabrication

This is lesser known among students and more a problem with scientists and others who publish data-driven analyses. There have been some high-profile cases in the last few years of professional scientists faking data for publication. It does exist though with undergrads, primarily in labs. It involves faking data from an experiment or inserting/removing "inconvenient" data points to achieve a predetermined result the data otherwise does not bear out. There are solid statistical methods to remove bad data, but these should be explained when you apply them. Students probably get away with this more than anything because most labs are done to get an answer that is usually not in doubt and usually graders do not question data that meets expectations. This is not to say it's okay, however. It's academic dishonesty just like everything else and can get you in hot water. It's often done if you can't get the lab to "work right." In this situation ask the TA for help.

The worst type of situation for data fabrication is if you're working in the lab of a professor on a research project or job. Here you are doing real research that could have a real impact on the world. Faking data could have huge implications such as disciplinary action for yourself and the professor, loss of grant money, and even loss of jobs. Never do it! Sometimes you may be under intense pressure from a researcher to get certain results. If this is the case and you can't alleviate it one-on-one with the principal investigator, inform someone else in the department. You may have to even leave the group entirely if you can't get them to change their behavior, but remember, if you lie with dogs you will get fleas. It's better not to be associated with unethical research.

Essential classes

Regardless of core courses, there are some classes you should consider taking if you need them:

1. Writing—good writing is a skill you can carry throughout your entire life. I was once a horrible writer but a writing course helped me do a complete 180-degree change.

2. Intro Science—there are a lot of intro science classes, even those for non-science majors. As problems become more complex and scientific knowledge becomes more important, this could help you in understanding many future developments.

3. Statistics—Everyone should know the basic concepts of statistics like mean, variance, sample size, etc. This can prevent you from being fooled or taken in by false statistics in the future.

4. Public Speaking—A course or club (like Toastmasters) should be on your list for at least a semester. If you want to go anywhere, public speaking is critical, and it's best to develop this in a non-threatening environment like college where your mistakes are quickly forgotten.

5. Formal Etiquette—Which sides do the knives and forks go on and which wine glasses are for red and white wine? You will likely end up at formal dinners in the future and understanding the etiquette is crucial. Pick this up if you can.

6. The Bill of Rights and U.S. Constitution—For Americans, this is something everyone should know. Your rights and the basic out-

line of American government are crucial to being an informed voter and citizen. Even if you only read them in the library, put this on your list.

There are many more to consider like personal finances, world geography, or world history. Look for classes that teach you important skills for life, even if they don't fall within your particular major.

Special majors and requirements

There are special situations in your academic career which I think merit special attention. I'll try to cover some examples below.

Freshman year, first semester

This is your first fling with college. It's also when most people screw themselves up. The joy of freedom from parents and rules and being surrounded by pretty people, parties, and alcohol can be a potent recipe for failure. Those who coasted through high school on EdCon 5 or 4 study habits will mistakenly apply them here, with horrific results.

The GPA damage that many do in their freshman year can take years to recover from. If you want to go to med school, you probably need a 3.5 GPA or higher. If you goof up and screw up in your first semester and get a 2.0, you'll need to make straight A's and have a 4.0 every semester with a full course load until the end of your sophomore year to make it back to 3.5. This will likely require continuous EdCon 2 or EdCon 1 study habits. Not a fun way to spend college. You'll soon find out that the hardcore pre-med classes like organic chemistry are hard to get A's in, so even if you do well in everything else, you may not get to 3.5 and above until the end of your junior year. Then guess what? It's time to apply to medical school along with the people who did not screw up and have 3.75 to 4.0 GPAs. Lots of people in this situation unfortunately give up on their dream to be doctors.

It's hard for many eighteen-year-olds to have perspective on how much their first year counts in determining their possible future. But it's real. You aren't going to have a 4.0 every semester most likely so the best way to prevent this scramble is to not screw up your first year.

Also, many people suffer from deflation syndrome. At their high school they were the smartest guy, top of their class. In college, it's a whole new ballgame. You may have your ego flattened and feel humbled. I know I did seeing the brilliance of some of the people I met. You'll find you aren't the best and brightest in some things or maybe nothing. This can be frustrating and depressing or even create a sense of inferiority. Don't let it.

Everyone is in college for different reasons. Your job is to perform and do well and achieve your goals. You don't have to be perfect or even the best in every situation. Realize you're in college for a reason and deserve to be there to accomplish your dreams. What everyone else is doing, even if they may send deprecating comments in your direction, should not impinge on your sense of worth.

Science and engineering

Math, science, and engineering have a deserved reputation for being tough. The subject matter is dense and complicated, and if you don't understand the basics you're never going to catch up. What's worse is that many departments, especially engineering, see their job as weeding out students. If you pass, you pass. If not, oh well. A lot of people start out wanting to be an engineer and end up with another major.

When you get to college, ask yourself if you really want to be a mathematician, engineer, or scientist. If so, you need to recognize the commitment and sacrifice involved. First, your study habits will unfortunately have a higher proportion of EdCon 2 and 1 than your friends in other majors. Engineering is often worse than math or most sciences as far as the workload. You have to accept this in order to compete. There are students in your classes from foreign countries who have worked their whole life for this opportunity and realize it may be their only chance to be middle class. They will study to succeed and break the curve. You need to prepare.

First, stop trying to keep up with everyone else in the social scene. If all of your friends are in a major with less work and want to party much more, you must set limits. If that doesn't work, be alone or hang out with people who understand. You can't allow peer pressure to derail you. Second, get tutoring your first semester from the beginning. You can't afford to slip up. Third, find a study group for classes in which you have difficulty or are known to be difficult. Once the group solves the problem, it will be easier for you to solve it on your own later.

In addition, you should bite the bullet and commit one weekend early in the semester to getting ahead in your main classes by at least a month.

Yes, a month (more than the two days I suggested earlier). If you don't know the homework, at least outline the chapters following the syllabus. Early in the semester the workload is lighter, which will make this possible. This may seem like a tall order but it pays dividends later. After committing this one weekend you should be able to comfortably do well with EdCon 3 habits until exam time or projects. Also, it will leave you more time to party and socialize in future weekends because you will never feel under the pressure to do EdCon 1.

In engineering again, there are a lot of projects, sometimes group projects. Always make sure you pull your own weight and contribute. You may have to deal with big egos and it's best not to react sharply but affirm your own worth and continue to work on being a valuable group member. If there's tension in the group you can't resolve, you may ask the professor to switch you to a different group. It's best to try to resolve differences one-on-one though with group members. Remember, not all engineers are the sociable types and may be trying to hide insecurities behind bombast. Not taking the bait will make you a better person and gain you the respect of others.

One last note, and this applies to pre-med and pre-law as well, is if you want to pledge for a fraternity, make sure you consider the time commitment it will require and whether it will damage your academic standing. I have nothing against fraternities and think overall they are great institutions but make sure the pledge process doesn't completely disregard academic concerns. It can be done and I know a guy that pledged Omega Psi Phi and went to an Ivy League medical school, but outside of pledging, all he did was study. If you can pledge any year, you may want to wait and get firmly established, even if it means pledging with underclassmen. If it never seems to work, pledge in graduate school or after you graduate. You can do this and the pledge process is often distilled to the essence of what the fraternity should truly be about.

Pre-med/pre-law

Graduate studies in medicine and law are becoming increasingly more difficult to get into due to high competition. In the United States university system, you're effectively competing against the best and brightest in the world so you need to prepare accordingly. First, for pre-med students. You need to do your best to ace all of the main required courses, especially in biology, chemistry, and physics. This is essential. A C in English does not look as bad as a C in biology for most med school admissions. You need to also realize that med schools look for high GPAs. You don't want to kill your schedule if it will inordinately affect your grades.

In addition, you need to prepare for MCATs as far in advance as possible. If you are taking mock MCATs a month before the real exam, it's too late. You should start taking trial exams, such as those you can get in test prep books, as soon as you have the required knowledge to understand all the questions, probably the end of your sophomore year. There should be no surprises when you walk in to take that test. If time and finances allow, a tutoring class like the Princeton Review or Kaplan can also help. There are also summer programs at schools like the University of Pennsylvania for pre-meds to help them prepare for medical school. When you finally take the MCATs you may want to take them for the first time in the fall or spring of your junior year so you can retake them in May or June if you don't get the score you want.

Also, make sure you can get internships or research opportunities if possible that look good on your résumé or help you reaffirm if medicine is right for you. Finally, before you do all of this, make sure you want to be a doctor for the right reasons. You'll spend at least four more years, not including residency, and tens of thousands of dollars in this pursuit. Not to mention the intense studying. Medicine is still a lucrative field, but it's often increasingly less so unless you're very specialized, so make sure more than money drives you.

Pre-law also has similar rigors, but you have a bit more flexibility in classes and majors. One thing you should do is take a class, often offered through the philosophy department, on logical analysis. This can include rhetoric, syllogisms, dilemmas, and other types of logical problems. This will be important to help you on the Law School Admission Test (LSAT) later. Like med school, grades can be important depending on where you want to go to. In addition, you may want to get involved with legal activities such as mock trial or legal societies. You should also keep up with key legal news such as court decisions and legal debates. Finally, though this may not help you get into law school, understanding how to search a legal library and use tools like Lexis-Nexis will be extremely helpful once you are in law school.

Foreign language classes

I once had an academic adviser in college who gave me great advice about languages: learning a language is like being pregnant, you go all the way or not at all. In line with this, if there's a foreign language requirement or if you want to learn a new language, make sure you budget at least four semesters to it to obtain any kind of proficiency.

Choosing a language is a personal decision. The most useful languages in the world right now for Americans are likely Spanish, Mandarin Chinese, and perhaps Arabic. All other languages such as French, German, Portuguese, Russian, and Japanese are very context specific, and while very useful in their countries, they're not much used elsewhere except French, which is spoken widely in Africa, and Portuguese, which is used in Brazil.

Once you commit to a language, you need to apply it outside of class or you'll never learn it. For example, if you're learning Spanish you should watch Univision or Telemundo for at least an hour several times a week. Watching the *telenovelas* or soap operas can be very instructive (and great eye candy). *Destinos* is an instructional Spanish show from PBS that is readily available as well. For other languages, with the advent of the Internet you can easily download shows through Peer-to-peer (P2P) software like eMule, watch on YouTube, or see streaming from major stations like Globo from Brazil. Since these are shows from other countries, you don't have to worry as much about copyright implications while in the United States.

Make sure you write down the words you don't know and make up sentences to aid in memorization. Though it may seem twisted, one technique that worked for me when I learned Chinese and Portuguese was to write sentences that were shocking, lurid, or weird to make the words stick in my mind. So to learn the word for television, instead of writing "I am watching television" I would write "I threw the television at my stupid neighbor." For some reason, the words always stuck better that way.

A final method to improve foreign language learning is to find a native speaker study partner. This should be a person who wants to improve their English language skills. You and this person can meet once or twice a week for an hour and converse for half an hour in their language and the other half in English. Some universities have a formal program that can match people. If not, ask or post a flyer looking for people. You can meet in a public place like a café or over dinner. One thing to be careful of is to make sure it stays equal. Both partners should benefit, so it should be half the time in each language. In addition to what we taught each other, my past language partners have become lifelong friends.

It is your choice whether this person should be a man or woman. It doesn't really matter, but you should know if you become romantically involved, contrary to what people think it may not help you learn the language better. Lots of times, once in a relationship people minimize friction by only using English (so one doesn't keep getting corrected) and the pressure to actually learn the language may diminish. I know a lot of people who tried to learn their girlfriend's or wife's language but eventually just gave up and used English.

Transferring schools

Some people find, for academic or other reasons, that they want to transfer schools. Sometimes this can be from a smaller school or community college to a better university or to a school where the academics are more up to your abilities and expectations. There is nothing shameful in this decision, but you need to focus on what the reason for transferring is.

If it's because of a transient reason like you miss your high school friends, hate your roommate, had a bad breakup, or had one bad semester, you may want to think twice. These types of things can happen at any school, so leaving for these reasons doesn't guarantee you won't encounter them again elsewhere. Also, make sure the reasons aren't an internal dissatisfaction such as everything not being "perfect" or just typical problems in adjusting initially. Otherwise, you may hop schools several times before you finally have to settle.

If you need to move, then do your research. See how many of your major credits will transfer and which classes you may have to redo. Also, what core courses does the new school require that you don't have? Second, realize that in transferring you may be lonelier, at least at first. Many people make their friends their freshman year and then lock into cliques that aren't always down with absorbing new people. If you're leaving the first school because you don't fit in socially, just realize there's no quick fix at a new school unless you already know people there.

As with applying to college, make sure you meet all deadlines and also inform the right people at your school of your plan to leave. This will ensure you don't get bills or notices that other continuing students are required to complete.

Conclusion

Academics are the foundation of your success in college and in the future. They are also crucial to your development as a person and a love of knowledge will keep you in good stead throughout your life.

Never forget that learning to educate yourself and seek your own understandings of things through the evidence and analysis is more important than grades. Thomas Jefferson once said, "if a nation expects to be ignorant and free in a state of civilization, it expects what never was and never will be." Learning to learn is the true freedom that can keep you liberated throughout your life.

Chapter 3
Finances

If you would be wealthy, says he, in another almanac, think of saving as well as of getting: the Indies have not made Spain rich, because her outgoes are greater than her incomes. Away then with your expensive follies, and you will not have so much cause to complain of...beware of little expenses; a small leak will sink a great ship.
—Benjamin Franklin, The Way to Wealth

Spend, spend, spend. Then call your parents. Repeat. This describes the limited financial knowledge and health of millions of college students. Sadly, much of our society is a promotion of spend-now-figure-out-how-to-pay-later behavior. Never before, except maybe before the financial crisis, have young people had such easy access to debt ranging from valid student loans to credit cards and other riskier types of loans. It is easy to get stuck. Perhaps you don't estimate your semester expenses correctly or it is too easy to swipe the plastic and let your mom worry about it. Either way, you need to become financially savvy. It is inexcusable when so many students graduate with their credit already destroyed by bad decisions, reckless spending, and false beliefs about how the financial world operates.

It is not a matter of work ethic, intelligence, or even educational training. There are many people who are expert accountants yet allow their life to be a financial wreckage. There is a lot to learn, but we can go through the basics that you should know during your college experience.

There are two main scopes of finance to which you need to be attentive during college. First are your educational finances and the options you can use to pay for your education. Second are your personal finances, which encompass everything from spending money, savings, car costs, etc. Both are important and both can impact your long-term credit scores and financial health. Before we begin to talk about strategies it helps if you have some basic financial literacy.

Quick guide to key financial concepts

For some, all of this may be new. For others, it can be a review that can be rapidly skimmed. In either case, make sure you firmly understand these concepts before going into college.

At the basic level are two concepts: net worth and income/expenses. Net worth is formally defined as your assets minus liabilities. Assets are things that you have that are cash or can be converted into cash. These range from the money in your bank account to a car you own and even property if you are fortunate enough to have it. Liability is basically another word for debt. These include student loans, credit cards, and auto loans if they are in your name. The vast majority of students have negative net worth. This is not necessarily bad since most students have very little assets to their names. However, there is a second dimension that is more important than the actual size of the debt. That is your ability to "service" or pay your debts.

All debt comes with payments. That's the price you pay for borrowing money. Every period, usually monthly, you are required to pay a minimum amount to pay down both part of the "principal," or the original amount that was borrowed, and the interest, which is a percentage of the principal that you pay as the cost of the loan. Student loan interest rates are typically in the range of a few percentage points. Credit card interest rates are typically described by the APR (annual percentage rate), which will be discussed in detail later. APR can typically be 15% or higher.

This brings us to your income and expenses. Your net income is your income minus expenses. Unlike net worth, which is a fixed value at any given point in time, income and expenses vary over time and you can measure them over a typical period such as a month or year. Of course, income is any money you receive whether it's from jobs, parents, scholarship disbursements, etc. Expenses are money you spend on living or school costs and paying for debt such as credit cards. Student loan debt payments are usually not due until at least six months after graduation. One misconception some people have is that receiving money from debt like credit cards is income. It increases your assets by buying you stuff, but it also increases your debts. It only delays expenses and also accrues additional interest.

When you include all your sources of income, your net income needs to be positive. Otherwise, you will have to build up more debt to get by. One way to keep track is to create a budget. You should know how much you get from jobs, your parents, or any other sources. You need to also estimate your expenses, and this will give you a good idea of what you should plan on spending. For example:

	Per Semester
Income	
Work Study	$2,000
Allowance	$3,000
Expenses	
Living	$1,000
School Fees (not covered by parents or loans)	$1,000
Discretionary (fun, etc.)	$1,000
Gas and Car Maintenance	$500
Credit Card Interest	$200
Net Income	$1,300

This is just an illustrative example, and it usually is hard to be so net positive during a typical semester. There are two things you need to realize. One, is to find a way to manage your expenses to keep your net income positive. Two, is to find a way to save money. A good rule is to save 10% of your gross income (total income without subtracting expenses). In the example above, it would be about $500.

Now we have some bare basics, we can discuss school expenses.

School expenses and financial aid

School fees are the first priority since if they aren't covered, you won't be in college for too long. They can typically be divided into a few main categories: tuition, room and board, meal plans, books, and other expenses. For all but the last two, the school will contact your family directly with billing statements if they are the designated payers for your education. Once the bills come, it is up to your family to decide how to pay. Most people do not have the full value needed lying around in savings so a variety of financial aid sources are often sought.

Financial aid falls into three main categories: grants and scholarships, loans, and work-study. The best are obviously grants or scholarships since these do not require any repayment or further work on your part. They can be difficult to come by, however. Loans are often necessary and will make up the bulk of many student financial aid awards. These are available from a variety of sources, including federal and state governments, private companies, or indirect sources such as home equity loans. Finally, work-study are jobs the federal government funds via a university. These are campus jobs that allow students to make some money, which they can use to help supplement other sources for their education.

Grants

Grants and scholarships are numerous but are unreliable until they are awarded. There are many scholarships and millions in scholarship money goes unawarded each year. However, this can be partially due to the fact that certain scholarships are for people of a certain ethnic or national origin, particular majors, or other specific criteria. One thing that many people do not realize is that the huge rush in applications for scholarships is by students in their senior year of high school. Once in college, the necessity to find funding is usually forgotten and the application rate goes down. You may find that applying for scholarships during college, particularly after choosing your major, is a more successful strategy.

Common sources for scholarships can include organizations tied to your major, school departments, or special foundations. As a student, you should be sure to join the national organization for your major/career to be eligible for any possible scholarships. In addition, search through the web and other sources to make sure you keep appraised of additional scholarships and opportunities that may come up.

There can also be grants from government sources. The federal government offers grants through the Pell Grant program. These grants, at a maximum of $5,500 per year at the time of writing, are available based on financial need for undergraduate students. In order to receive a Pell Grant as well as federal loans, you and your parents are required to fill-out and file a Free Application for Federal Student Aid (FAFSA) form which is typically due on June 30 each year. In addition, you have to sign up for the Selective Service (the national draft registry). There are additional grants available based on need such as the Federal Supplemental Educational Opportunity Grant (FSEOG) for those with exceptional financial need as well as grants for military veterans.

Students may have access to state funding as well. Residents of Georgia can use the HOPE Scholarship to pay tuition at public colleges if they meet the requirements. Other states sometimes have similar programs.

Loans

Loans have, by and large, become the chief source of aid for many people who do not pay directly for their education. Loans typically come from the federal government or private sources. As stated before, loans have both a principal (amount of money borrowed) and interest (cost of borrowing) component. Student loans typically do not require payout until after graduation, but by then the principal will have accumulated to a large amount. Student loans are also special in that they are a class of debt, which you cannot eliminate or reduce through personal bankruptcy unless you can prove undue financial hardship. In personal bankruptcy, you can negotiate with most creditors for the reduction or elimination of debt though it will severely damage your credit history. Student loans, like child support, are an exception to this, and you have to convince a judge they are a special burden. Not a reliable strategy.

Loans are available from federal, sometimes state, school, and private sources. Federal loans are the most common and sought after. The most well known are the Perkins, Direct Stafford, and Direct PLUS loans. Like Pell Grants, all three loans are only available after filling out FAFSA forms. Perkins and Direct Stafford loans are offered directly to students for undergraduate study. Typically they both max out at the same amount per year as a Pell Grant—$5,500—though the Direct Stafford can increase over time. Your total loan burden for each is limited to about $30,000 for your entire school enrollment. These numbers do change so check what the limit is before you apply. All federal loans are guaranteed by the federal government against default. This does not mean you can just decide not to pay, but rather that the federal government is able to allow lending based only on need and to stabilize interest rates.

What is the difference then? Perkins loans are loaned from the university, though they are directly subsidized by the federal government. They have an interest rate set at 5%. Stafford loans are direct to students through the Department of Education though the originator is a university or sometimes a private company. Stafford loans can also be subsidized or unsubsidized. Subsidized loans are based off financial need in an amount determined by your school and carry a lower interest rate. You are not charged interest on these loans while at school since the federal government pays for the interest.

Unsubsidized Stafford loans are also determined by the school but do not require proof of financial need. However, interest begins accruing immediately, even while you are still in school.

Stafford loan interest rates vary by school year. For 2012–13, they are fixed at 6.8%, which is higher than the Perkins loan. For a brief period in the past, the rates were below 5%. Also, Stafford loans have origination (processing fee) fees and guarantee fees (insurance against student default) that range from 1% to 3% of the principal. Stafford loans are by far the larger source of money and should be available whenever you file the FAFSA. Perkins loans are more limited and are typically on a first-come, first-serve basis so it is important to file your FAFSA paperwork as soon as possible to get access to Perkins loans.

People typically say Perkins is better because of the (usually) lower interest rate and lack of origination and guarantee fees. It is also more limited and much harder to get access to. In any case, both have limits on the amount you can borrow and typically, Perkins has a ten-year time limit to pay back. Stafford can be extended for decades more, so there is less pressure to pay it off immediately. A final option is for parents only. The federal Direct PLUS loan allows parents to borrow as much as they need to pay for their child's education. The loans are not need based, and parents can borrow up to the total amount of schooling fees minus all other received financial aid. Interest rates are higher at around 8%, and payments begin sixty days after the money is disbursed. Origination fees are also high at 4%, though 1.5% is rebated if the first twelve months are paid on time. One big downside is that receiving such a loan depends on your family's credit history. Like all other federal loans, this needs FAFSA filled out.

When federal financial aid is not enough, there are sources at the state level in some states. For example, in Massachusetts the Massachusetts Educational Finance Authority provides fixed-rate loans for state residents at slightly higher interest rates. Other states have similar programs, so check your state to see what's available. When state sources fail though, you can go to private lenders.

Private loans

Private lending is the latest evolution in the education financing/loan market. Almost non-existent fifteen years ago, they've become huge a source of funding as costs of schooling have sky-rocketed.

TABLE 1: Comparison of loan types; Note total of unsubsidized and subsidized Stafford loans cannot exceed the unsubsidized maximum.

Loan Type	2012-13 School Year Typical Rate	Maximum borrowing amount (year)	Maximum borrowing amount (total)
Perkins	5.0%	$5,500	$27,500
Stafford (Subsidized)	6.8%	$3.5k-$5.5k depending on the school year	$23,000
Stafford (Unsubsidized)	6.8%	$5.5k -$7.5k for dependent students; $9.5k-$12.5k for independent students	$31,000 (dependent); $57,500 (independent); total of unsubsidized and subsidized
Direct PLUS (parents)	7.9%	The cost of school - received aid	The cost of school - received aid
Private	varies; fixed or variable	determined by lender	determined by lender

As I'll explain when discussing these loans, you should make sure to exhaust all possible grants, federal loans, and state loans before you seek out a private educational loan. In short, they cost more, are even more impossible to discharge if you go bankrupt, and some have dangerous provisions.

A private loan can be offered by many companies from those that specialize in undergraduate lending to larger corporations such as Citibank. A private loan is like any other educational loan. It has a principal and an interest rate and a typical term. However, private educational loans have several aspects that make them much different from federally guaranteed loans like Perkins and Stafford. First, you apply to the private lender directly. You don't need to either to fill out a FAFSA form or apply through the school, however, the school may have to certify you are a student with a minimum course burden for eligibility purposes. Second, your ability to qualify as well as the interest rate depends heavily on your credit or your parents' credit if they apply. In addition, the interest rate not only depends on your credit, higher rates for bad credit, the interest rate on most private loans is variable, not fixed. Third, you almost always need a co-signer if you are taking out the loan as a student. A co-signer, usually your parent or guardian, is someone who guarantees that they will pay for the loan in case you default.

In addition to the above, private loans have origination fees and are even more difficult to get rid of than federal loans if you default or go into bankruptcy. If the federal government ever announces a partial loan forgiveness for the heavily indebted regarding federal loans, which is likely in the future, private loans will not qualify. These reasons and more are why private loans should be a final option.

Regarding the costs, private loans are typically several percentage points above the federal loan rate. As stated earlier, their interest rates are variable. Like some of the infamous variable rate mortgages that sunk homeowners in the foreclosure crisis, you need to read the loan terms carefully to make sure you are not sunk. A typical interest rate structure on a private loan is the London Interbank Offered Rate (LIBOR) plus a profit percentage. The profit percent ranges from 2% to 9% on most loans.

The LIBOR rate is like the loan interest rate for big banks, specifically those in London. Since big banks have lots of cash, they are considered to (usually) have good credit and get the lowest (LIBOR) rate on average. All of us little people have less cash and so pay higher interest rates on loans, but the LIBOR is considered the "bottom" or starting point for calculating our interest rates. There are different LIBOR rates for loans of different terms, but the most common for student loans is the one-month LIBOR, which as of March 2012 is about 0.24%. This sounds great if you can get a low rate of LIBOR plus 2%. However, 5% is a more likely average rate.

However, there are several things you must be cautious of. First, this is a variable rate and despite cheap money from central banks to help the economy, you should assume LIBOR will increase 2% to 3% over the life of the loans. If you can't pay at a rate of 3% higher, you should not take out the loan. Second, there is currently a scandal regarding LIBOR where banks were manipulating the reported LIBOR numbers down since a higher LIBOR would indicate banks see one another as more of a credit risk. Therefore, as this clears out, LIBOR will likely increase, possibly substantially. Some loans use the Wall Street Journal Prime Rate instead, which is an American measure related to LIBOR. It is typically higher—around 3.25% in March 2012—but those with good credit can get lower rates such as Prime Rate plus 0.20%. On the high end though, you can get Prime Rate plus 7% or more!

In addition there are fees for originating the loan that are usually a percentage of the principal. Many people erroneously look only at the interest rate without taking origination fees into account. A quick rule of thumb is every 3% to 4% of origination fees you have to pay are equivalent to another 1% on the loan interest rate. So calculating the true rate of the loan can be the exercise of LIBOR plus profit percent plus origination fee percent divided by three. While you may not have to repay the loan until graduation, the interest still accumulates and will be in your subsequent payments. Recently, some companies have introduced fixed rate loans though they require more stringent credit requirements and typically start at a higher rate.

This still may not be your final interest rate, however. Many loans have special fine print that allows them to increase your interest rate if you miss a payment. Even one payment! Therefore you must read the financial print very carefully and if necessary, get help from the student aid office or someone else with knowledge of these financial instruments. Late payments are generally not a good idea since your credit score as well as the credit score of your co-signer can be damaged by multiple missed payments or large delinquent balances.

A final note on private loans is to beware of fraudulent or too good to be true deals. First, private loans are not subsidized by the government so it is virtually impossible for them to be cheaper than a federal loan. There are exceptions if you or your parent has outstanding credit but the rate is still variable. If you see a rate that seems lower than the rate for a federal loan, watch out! There is likely something strange here. Students are still dealing with the suspicious and unethical practices homeowners dealt with during the height of the housing bubble and the mortgage fraud debacle. Variable rate loans, provisions to hike rates due to late payments, and other terms can combine to form powerful "gotchas" if you are ever in a financial bind. Also, many student loans are packaged and resold as derivative securities much like mortgages are packaged together into mortgage backed securities. If the student loan default rate ever spikes, these could go sour and severely restrict the credit available for student borrowers.

Some companies are downright out to defraud students and earn as much money as possible in the process. If you ever have suspicions about a student loan company, ask your financial aid office. Some universities like UCLA have a list of approved private student lenders. It's good to start with lenders from lists like these since they've proven they are more reliable.

Student loans have become the largest source of funding for education. In addition, with the rising cost of education and the borrowing limits for federal loans, private lenders forcefully stepped into the gap, sometimes with high interest rates. As of February 2012, the Federal Reserve Bank of New York estimates that the average student borrower has $23,300 in student loan debt. A better measure, the median, indicates an average debt burden of $12,800, which is lower than the average since there are some people with massive ($100,000-plus) amounts of student debt. In addition, because of the hard economic times and the large sums, many people are falling behind. The same source estimates more than 27% of student lenders are delinquent on their payments. This can extract a huge toll on your credit score and financial stability.

Black students are the ethnic group most dependent on loans for studying costs, according to the Department of Education. The National Center for Education Statistics, National Postsecondary Student Aid Survey (1993–2008) estimates the number of Black students using student loans jumped from under 5% to almost 25% over this period. Student loans can place a heavy burden on any student's financial future, and defaults can destroy your credit.

In summary, remember the following tips:

1. The first recourse is any savings you or your parents have accumulated to pay for your education.

2. Exhaust all federal, state, or school grants and scholarship opportunities before seeking out loans.

3. When looking at loans, prioritize first the Perkins (apply early), then Stafford, and finally your parents can see if a Direct PLUS loan is right for them.

4. Private student loans are a last resort to be used only if necessary.

One final loan topic is about loan refinancing and alternative ways of paying such as home equity loans. Refinancing a federal loan with a private loan is usually not a good idea. Though the private loan may have a low interest rate if the reference rate like LIBOR is low, it may rapidly rise if rates change. In addition, it is easier to get debt forgiveness for federal loans than private loans if the loan payments become a financial hardship. You can get some consolidation and refinancing through the federal Direct loans program. If you have multiple loans, prioritize paying off the private ones first unless the federal ones are due sooner. This relieves the heavier burden first.

Some families have been using home equity loans to finance their children's education. This can be a way to get money, but it is not recommended except if there are no other options, including equivalent schools that are less expensive. If taken out, it should only be for a low percentage of a house's value, such as 25%. Though the burden is on your parents and you can get a higher value loan easier with a loan secured by housing collateral, it puts the house on the line if they ever go into default. In addition, there is always the possibility of the loan going underwater if the price of the house plummets.

How drugs can kill your financial aid

If you want to make sure you continue to get federal financial aid, it's a good idea to stay away from drugs. If you're convicted of a drug offense at any time while you are receiving federal financial aid, you could lose it. If the conviction is overturned or set aside you could be clear, but if the conviction stands, there's a high chance you could lose your aid for at least a year.

The penalties for possession are lighter than those for dealing. For first time conviction of possession you lose aid eligibility for a year. For the second offense you lose aid for two years. You could easily end your federal financial aid from a freshman-year conviction. The dealers have it even worse. If you are convicted of dealing any amount you will lose aid eligibility for two years. The second conviction for dealing ends federal aid forever. For solely possession, three or more convictions also end your aid eligibility forever. Forever isn't permanent since there are options like rehabilitation programs and drug testing that can make you eligible again, but by the time the paperwork clears, you may be done. Why roll the dice?

Just remember, if you are going to puff or deal, any pleasure or money you make is weighed against the thousands you could lose in financial aid. Keep your eyes on the prize and leave it alone.

Additional costs

School is the big cost and likely includes tuition, housing options, meal plans, and books. There are other costs to life, however, and you must budget for these.

Meals

Freshmen are likely forced to have a meal plan. It is usually a combination of cafeteria meals per week and some sort of point credits that allow you to eat at non-cafeteria and local food establishments. Meal plans are typically not a bargain but add a lot of convenience. Once you begin to learn more about your options, you can make choices to eat healthier or cheaper.

Only you know how much you eat, but the easiest way to save money is preparing your own food and not eat out as much—be it vending machines or restaurants. You may be a guy but learning some of your mom's best easy recipes can pay dividends if you have a kitchen in your dorm or apartment. If not, the easiest option is to make your own lunch. This can save you over thirty dollars per week, which can be a couple of hundred dollars a semester. Not small change. It also makes you more flexible on the go when you have a sandwich, piece of fruit, and chips. For those on a budget, this is definitely an option to consider.

If you cook dinner, you will likely not have time every night. The best option is on Sunday night, or another free night during the week, to cook four or five servings of a meal so you can refrigerate it and eat it throughout the week by just heating it up. This can help you control your diet and reduce the time and money you have to spend.

For the really budget conscious, you can help control impulse buying by going to the grocery store less. How do you accomplish this? Plan out for several weeks or months in advance what you'll have for dinner and maybe breakfast and lunch. Break down those recipes into their individual items and make one big buy at the store. It may put you out of one hundred to two hundred dollars in one hit, but you will save more in the long run by not visiting the store as often and buying twenty to forty dollars on impulse buys here and there. If you like snacks, buy the bulk-size granola bars or whatever you like to take in your backpack.

Living

Living on or off campus is an important choice. For some the question is the cost, others convenience, and still others, privacy. You must do a detailed comparison of costs before you move though. Some people naively compare their dorm rate per semester with the rental rate for an off-campus apartment and feel they are getting a steal. However, in the dorms you do not have to pay for utilities or trash collection separately. An apartment may require those things, and you must ask the landlord the average monthly cost for these items and add them to the rent.

If you get digital cable, TiVo and other amenities you can't have in a dorm, this will raise the price as well. You will also be responsible for certain upkeep that you can't call the maintenance staff for though your landlord should handle the repairs. Some landlords require cosigners as well since students have little income or credit history. Sometimes living with friends can reduce the cost but each party must be responsible and pay their rent on time. Otherwise, you can all suffer. Strains of cleaning up after others and living together have also hurt many otherwise good friendships. Sometimes the best friends are close but not too close!

Cars

The full costs of cars will be covered in Chapter 8, but rest assured this will be a sizable financial burden when you include parking permits, gas, necessary maintenance, insurance, and title registration. Make sure you realistically take all of these into account.

Fun

You need to budget money to have fun. College isn't about living as a hermit. That means money to eat out, go on dates, have fun with your friends, etc. If you successfully save in the other areas, you should be able to have enough money to have reasonable fun without worrying about every penny you spend.

Credit cards

You will see them the second you get on campus. Hordes of fellow students at tables offering free T-shirts, water bottles, and instant credit. Most people entering college are a financial blank slate—no credit history and every opportunity to build a great financial backbone or cause themselves great damage. First of all, if you think you are winning by getting a five-dollar T-shirt in exchange for signing up for a credit card, you obviously don't know the game. At 15% annual interest you only need to carry a balance of $400 for one month for them to make that back.

Many students don't understand the purpose and peril of credit cards and are quickly sucked into a situation of additional debt they cannot control. Credit cards can be complicated in their actual terms, depending on the type of card and the fine print, but there's a basic model that can help you understand how to use most credit cards. To understand the concept of credit cards, you must understand them for what they are, not what you want them to be. Credit cards are a high-interest loan. They can be a convenient high-interest loan but they are still a loan. First, credit cards should never be used to extend your spending power. The biggest mistake most students make is thinking a card with a high limit automatically makes them a bigger consumer. The payday will come sooner or later. Second, you should have no more than two credit cards in order to reduce the temptation to spend and limit your debt burden. It is best to start with one.

Credit cards will be coming to you fast and furious. They will come by campus salespeople, by mail, even by email. You can have a regular credit card from your bank, one from your favorite department store, one from your chosen airline, etc. Repeat after me: There is no reward for signing up for a credit card that is greater than how much the card will cost you. Otherwise the reward would make no business sense. Never sign up for a card because of the reward or signing bonus be it free money, free stuff, or store points.

Your first credit card should be used only for special large purchases or in emergencies where you are short on needed cash. If you are in a bind and need to make a payment where cash is not available or accepted, these can come in handy. If handled responsibly and paid on time, it can help build a great credit history that will serve you well. A second card can give you more flexibility, for example between card types like Visa, Mastercard, American Express, or Discover. It can also be good to get points for travel options like airlines.

If you use this card for non-emergencies, be sure you can pay the full balance each month. If not, you are spending too much money on the card. In order to understand the impact of the credit card, you must understand the concepts of the card's annual percentage rate (APR) and your average daily balance (ADB). APR is the effective annual interest rate on the credit card. It usually ranges between 15% to 20% and will typically include credit card fees. It also can be reported in two ways—as a "nominal" or "effective" rate. Nominal APR is the monthly interest rate times twelve while effective APR, the more accurate number, includes compounded interest, where interest is paid on interest for past unpaid balances.

Your monthly interest payment is usually calculated by dividing the APR by twelve and multiplying this times your ADB, which is the average amount of money you have outstanding on your card each month. This illustrates one strategy for reducing your monthly interest payment—paying down your credit card balance early. By doing this, you reduce the average amount on the card even though your total spending is the same. Your minimum monthly payment is the interest charge as calculated above plus a portion of the principal.

Many people are tempted to get by paying the minimal balance due. Never, ever do this if at all possible. By allowing your payments to roll over for another month you are paying interest on the balance again. For a nominal 15% APR, the monthly interest rate is 1.25%, so for every $100 on your ADB, you are throwing away $1.25. This may sound small, but if you only pay the minimum or fail to pay at all, after a year you will have paid $15 for every $100 you spent. At $1,000 this is $150, which could have bought a lot of pizza! It also will not help your credit history if you only pay minimum balances, especially if you go delinquent. In addition, like private student loans, some credit cards can reserve the right to raise the APR if you miss payments.

Another frequently obsessed-about option is the credit limit. Unless a limit for a card is unreasonably low, you should not choose a card, especially with a higher interest rate, for a higher credit limit. For reasonable spending, your credit limit should not be the limiting factor. In fact, you should restrain your spending and pay on time in order to improve your credit, which eventually increases your credit limit.

If you don't trust yourself with a credit card, don't get one. It's better to scrape by on cash than to live the good life that will come back to haunt you with a credit card. If you find yourself unable to pay off the monthly balance, rely on your parents to pay the balance in addition to the typical money they send you, or are tempted to buy things you know you can't afford, get rid of the card. Since identity theft or unauthorized charges can be an issue, you should shred credit cards in a shredder when disposing of them.

Bank accounts

When you set up a bank account on campus, it's best to choose a bank that's relatively accessible and has a convenient number of ATM locations. There aren't too many differences between large banks these days though some schools have university credit unions that may offer special perks. In the end, for the basic student, there are only a few differentiators.

First are fees. What kind of fees does the account have? Is there a minimum balance in order to waive an account maintenance fee? Finally, look at overdraft protection fees and maximum overdraft amounts. Overdrafts can happen though you should keep an eye on your account and checks to prevent this.

Generating income

Now that we've talked about responsible spending, we can discuss the other side of the equation: creating income. This is obviously the more difficult of the two but an essential skill. Many if not most of you will work during college in order to pay your bills or generate additional money. There are many types of jobs, and unfortunately with the current hard economic times, they are becoming scarcer and more competitive. While the overall unemployment for the entire U.S. population is 10%, for men aged sixteen to nineteen, it hovers around 20%-plus or 30%-plus for Black men.

The first types of jobs many people run into are work-study. These are offered through the school and typically pay at or slightly above minimum wage (the federal minimum wage was $7.25 as of press; some states have higher minimum wages). The total income you can receive from the job is limited and your maximum hours per week are limited to forty. These can be good first college jobs and maybe all you need to cover expenses and school. They range from library jobs, food services, IT, or other office jobs around the university. The library jobs are often most coveted being generally low stress, and you have a lot of down time where you can study. Generally more skilled jobs pay higher wages so working in IT administration or a similar job can pay more but they typically max out around $10 to $12 an hour. As a brief rule of thumb, for every ten hours you work per week at $10 per hour, you make $400 per month pre-tax withholdings.

There are other jobs on campus besides just work-study that will not limit your total annual income. However, their hourly wage rates are likely not to be much higher unless you have a special skill. Many students opt for jobs off campus. These can range from typical jobs waiting tables or working in customer service to temp positions such as those offered by temporary labor firms like Manpower or call centers. The best job for you depends on time commitments, availability, and possible career aspirations. When looking at salaries, especially in food service, you need to make sure you count tip income (or lack thereof) as part of your calculation of earnings. For example, waiting tables gets you tips, catering does not.

Second, if you need a job, don't look down on jobs that include manual labor. There are lots of jobs such as working with contractors, painting, or even trades (if you have time or money to learn) that can provide valuable business experience and build good contacts. Even if you are stuck in a job you hate, realize it is income until you can find better options. By doing the best you can at the job you can leave your employer with a good impression and maybe even a referral. I am not advocating taking abusive or discriminatory bosses but in today's labor market the best way to keep your job safe is to make yourself an asset.

One way to improve your work (and relieve boredom) is to learn the cutting edge of your business well. These days, almost every job or industry has an association that publishes a magazine. For example, if you have a "dead-end" job at a pizza joint, try subscribing to *Pizza Today*, which is the national magazine of the pizza industry. It could help you understand the bigger context of the industry. If you understand how the best pizza shops operate or what the trends are, you could approach your supervisor and ask to pilot a possible new initiative or product. This could demonstrate initiative and also help you learn the full operational and financial side of the business much better. Even if your boss isn't the kind to take advice, it can help you improve your own performance or make you more marketable to other jobs in the future. For bonus points, read the publications before your interview and really shock the manager who probably has never heard much beyond "I need a job."

For those who are lucky, they can find a job that fits their career aspirations perfectly. Be it a research position, a job at a hospital, or work in programming, these are great additions to your résumé. I was interested in IT and a job as the online advertising manager with the school newspaper brought me both commission income and great industry knowledge. With any job, make sure you guide your own career. If you have an aspiration for a certain position, even in a fast food restaurant, write it down and begin to make plans on how to achieve it.

A hidden golden opportunity for making money given your talents is tutoring. Tutors can charge relatively high hourly rates and have consistent business if they tutor for a hard or essential class. For example, most engineers need to pass computer science and pre-med students must pass organic chemistry. If you are good at this, it can be an easy money maker and get you $15 or more an hour. The main issues are both marketing so your ser-

vices are known and the seasonality of tutoring.
Fliers and perhaps announcements by professors
are a good way to get your tutoring services out
there. Tutoring is often seasonal because most
people rush to get it before midterms and finals
making business very good then, but taper off in
the period in between. One way to improve this is
to tutor in more than one subject to draw more
people. Another way, if you are a good negotiator
and money is available, is ask the department or
another organization like the Office of Black Affairs if they can sponsor you as a free tutor. You get
a lower hourly rate and maybe more workload
since you are now free to the students, but the income is consistent.

Entrepreneurship

A final option for job seekers can be entrepreneurship. This can be extremely rewarding but also
extremely difficult. Starting your own business is
not a small endeavor, and if you think it will allow
you to work less hours for the same money, you
need to think twice. Entrepreneurs are always on
call and must do everything they can to gain the
respect of their customers and increase business.

Being an entrepreneur can be as simple as
some of the perennial—but often extremely effective—side hustles such as cooking food, cutting or
doing hair, or promoting/throwing parties. However, no matter how big or small, a little bit of
planning can help make any business venture
much more organized, successful, and profitable.

If you decide to be an entrepreneur, the first
thing you must do is write a business plan. There
are many guides online on how to do this, but it is

essential that you write out your clear goals and realistically estimate possible income and expenses. You may find the income, while attractive, does not match the outlays of money to get started. Once you've done this, go to a business professor or local entrepreneur to get a quick review of the business plan to see if it is good. Some towns have non-profit organizations to help entrepreneurs called "business incubators" that offer this kind of support. Next, you are ready to get started.

You can just do business as a sole proprietor where your business is essentially tied to you as an individual. However, you are directly exposed to all risks. What you may want to do is apply to set up your own corporation to limit personal risk. You must understand the organization and taxation of the different types such as C corporations, S corporations, or limited liability corporations (LLC). For example, C corporations are taxed twice—once on corporate income and then again on any profit you take out, which is taxed as your personal income.

Once you have a corporation set up, you'll likely also want to purchase minimal business insurance. This can help provide important coverage in case of loss. You also want to check any state regulations. For example, if you are cooking food or cutting hair, you want to be familiar with minimal sanitary guidelines and any licensing you may need to operate as a legal business.

If you have any employees, make sure you handle their payments legally. Tax penalties for not withholding the right amount of taxes on employees are one of the biggest causes of business bankruptcy. What would be easiest is to use a company like Paychex to pay any employees you have. Speaking of taxes, you must always pay your taxes and report income and expenses honestly. If you have any contractors you've paid, make sure to file 1099-MISC forms as required in reporting their income and provide them with a copy.

For any business, marketing is often as important as the service provided. Sometimes marketing is more important. The first thing you should do is have business cards made. If you want them to be attractive, you may need to pay or have a friend design one for you. No one will use you unless you get your name out there. There are many lower budget options from fliers to social media that can help get your message out. Great ideas for all types of business marketing and business in general can be found in magazines such as *Entrepreneur* and *Fast Company*. In addition to marketing, do market research and make sure you know what the opportunities are and what customers want. This includes service requirements, pricing, and your competition. You must always have a strategy to beat the competition. Otherwise, who would use you?

Being your own boss can be liberating, but often it is also very stressful. The buck stops with you and you will think about the business 24/7. Lastly, remember to pay yourself. If you put in twenty hours a week and only net $100, you are effectively earning under minimum wage. In this situation, you need to find out how to improve the business sales and operations or consider if it is actually worth it to you.

Taxes

A final note: When you have income you must file taxes if you earn over a certain amount. An IRS publication called 501 has the details, but typically it's about $5,800 if you are a single person considered a dependent by your parents or $9,500 if you aren't. Form 1040 is the basic but you may need help from your parents or a financial advisor to see any special tax credits such as those from the American Opportunity Credit, a tax credit you can get in exchange for community service, that you are eligible for.

Financial fraud and identity theft

In this digital age, financial transactions through electronic mediums are increasingly common. The downside of this is that an unscrupulous individual or individuals can obtain one's personal information and use it to steal money, impersonate someone else for the purpose of committing fraud or getting credit cards, and even use your identity as a front for a serious crime. Identity theft has become so common, it should be a part of financial literacy.

Protecting yourself from identity theft is getting harder, but there are some simple steps you can take to eliminate the majority of problems. First, never divulge personal information such as your date of birth, social security number, passport number, or anything else to anyone who contacts you via phone or email. Your bank, insurance, or university will *never* contact you via email and ask for personal information. If someone calls you requesting this information, politely thank them, get their name, hang up and call the institution back from their official number on the back of your card or from the website. When calling directly you can be sure the person is who they say they are. Never send personal information over email. If it is someone you trust, like an employer, ask to fax the information or mail it and request they dispose of it or securely store it after receipt.

Some offers on campus will ask you to sign up and divulge this information. Again, it is a risk, and do not feel pressured to provide anything on the spot. Take the information with you and say you will fill it out later, then check out the source to make sure it is legit. Remember, read the forms carefully. Except for things like credit cards or bank accounts you are never obligated to give your social security number unless they have to do a credit check. If in question, ask if you can leave it off or use some alternate identification number. You will usually find out it is optional.

When disposing of sensitive material like statements, checks, or credit card statements, it's best to have a shredder on hand. A small one can be had for $25 at WalMart or perhaps you can find one on campus. Cutting them up with scissors is also an option, though much less effective, but you have to make sure the sensitive information like your name, address, and social security number are shredded. The possibility such a document can get in the hands of an unscrupulous person is relatively low, but the expenses of cleaning up identity fraud can be very high.

Finally, if you ever suspect you're being suckered into a scam, check the Federal Trade Commission website through Google and type in the

details or company name. Often scams are reported and you can find out if you're in danger. Remember, your personal financial data is very important and should only be divulged to trusted
parties. You have too much to worry about at
school without the harrowing experience of identity fraud.

Conclusion

Your financial health is an important yet often
neglected aspect of your well-being in college. Understanding your own personal finances is one of
the most important steps toward becoming an
adult. This is a lifelong learning process and this
chapter just scratches the surface, but it's one that
can mean the difference in your entire life.

Chapter 4
Relationships

Associate yourself with people of good quality, for it is better to be alone than in bad company.
—Booker T. Washington

Many of you will probably look at the title of this chapter and the first thing that comes to mind is women, but the relationships you'll have in college stretch far beyond that. Relationships, broadly defined, are the interactions you have with everyone you meet from the casual, to the roommate, to lovers and everything in between. Managing college is very much about managing relationships, and despite the heavy early focus on academics, failing at managing relationships almost precludes you from full success at college.

In fact, if you don't use your time at college to build valuable relationships and networking skills I can guarantee you'll be impairing yourself in future personal and professional relationships. The old saying, "it's not what you know but who you know" is as true in the twenty-first century as 2000 B.C., and while it does not imply everyone should be your friend, you must be adept at managing relationships to succeed.

The relationships start the second you find out who your roommate is and continue for decades after graduation, probably until the end of your life. Here, we will discuss the various types of relationships you will encounter. Don't worry, we will discuss the women as well.

97

Roommates

When you get on campus as a freshman, one of the first people you will meet is your roommate. Dorm life is going to be a significant part of your day, so your roommate is someone important to understand. You may be able to contact your roommate before matriculation. Sometimes colleges will send out the names and emails so the two of you can get acquainted. If so, it is good to drop a quick email and say hi. Maybe you can even become Facebook buddies. Though you haven't met yet, you can already help set up a cooperative relationship. Maybe your dorm is unfurnished and everyone needs to bring stuff. To save money and prevent overlap, break down what each of you will bring for the room. In college I brought the giant fan and a halogen lamp while my roommate brought the TV/VCR combo and fridge. However you want to work it out this can help you begin a cooperative relationship before you ever meet.

Once on campus, meet the person and get to know him. You can discuss backgrounds, families, commonalities, etc. You will also have differences though these won't come out immediately. The first weeks with your roommate are like the first dates with a girl—everyone puts up a front to make themselves look good. For many people, the first things they want to do are set ground rules and personal space. I wouldn't try to do too much up-front though basic expectations should be discussed. For example, start small like agreeing to keep the dorm clean, take turns taking out the trash, or having rules on playing music loud. If there are any shared expenses, you should specify up front how they will be split. The final important thing you should do is set up a dispute resolution mechanism. For example, if one of you has a problem, what is the best way to bring it up and agree to resolve it? This will allow you to not worry about specifying a bunch of rules up front and be able to successfully deal with situations as they come.

Once you respect each other it is easier to deal with other issues as they come up. If he likes staying up late and this disturbs you, it's easier to bring it up in the context of a solid relationship built on small steps rather than blowing up and risking being perceived as a prick. You do have the right to set red lines though. Further, if you wake up constantly to your roommate screwing some girl while you are in the room, you have the right to address this. Being unsanitary, rude, extreme violations of personal space, or otherwise being unaccommodating are also some things most people get tired of pretty quickly. The best thing to do is to bring it up politely the first time it happens instead of bottling it up and exploding at the next small infraction. If you come from a homogenous hometown community, you are about to find out about a world full of people with different ethics, morals, upbringings, and tolerances to what you may find annoying. Keep this in mind.

At times, you may have a roommate who disturbs you up front. Maybe they are a bit crazy, have annoying habits, or even have diametrically opposite political viewpoints. If it is the beginning of the semester, try to get to know the person and see if your initial perceptions were perhaps too harsh. Sometimes people can be much different than your first impression indicates. I have a friend who went to school down South and found out when he moved in that his roommate had a Confederate flag. Some people would have panicked or taken the guy to task for being offensive. Luckily he took the high ground and got to know the guy. Granted, they never agreed on the flag, but his roommate was a nice, kind, and upstanding person so the flag really never got in the way of having a good freshman year.

The three biggest issues I have typically seen flare up with roommates are noise, cleanliness, and visitors. These can typically sour a relationship, even if the person is relatively amicable. If they are blasting rap or heavy metal and you want to sleep or study, there is little room for compromise. Granted you could study in the library but you shouldn't feel unwelcome in your own room. Cleanliness is another big pet peeve and can range from dirty laundry on the floor to spoiled food not being discarded. Again, you both have responsibility for the room so you shouldn't be the only one to have to clean up after each night of Chinese food. You should also not be the offender, even if this was okay in the household in which you grew up. Finally, visitors can be a huge issue. Whether staying up all night talking, playing video games, having sex, or just being annoying, you should indicate that after a certain hour they should hang out somewhere else.

There may be situations though when you need to get a new roommate. If a roommate, despite repeated pleadings to change behavior, threatens your academic performance, health, or safety then you have the right to switch. First, discuss this with your RA if you feel comfortable doing so. He could provide valuable advice and put things in perspective if he thinks you are overreacting. If the situation does not improve, even with RA intervention, then it is time to get the paperwork done. In this case you should go to the administration and find out the steps to initiate a roommate switch. Once you have determined this is your course of action, let your roommate know and indicate you think you would live better somewhere else. If he threatens you or retaliates then you can use your RA or campus security to help you get out of the situation.

If you have repeated issues with roommates, you may want to ask yourself if you are part of the problem. Introspection is never easy, and there are no quick-and-fast rules, but one should always take into account one's own culpability in any situation. If you are introverted, which I am to an extent, you should angle for a single room after your freshman year and get rid of the roommate worries for good.

Friends and peer groups

Freshman year is the best and easiest time to meet people on campus. Typically you all are new and are distant from many if not most of your previous social and family relationships. People are open to meeting new friends and have not yet coalesced into cliques. There is no one way to meet and greet. In particular, you should attend as many of the freshmen welcome events as you can once on campus. It's best if you're not shy and feel free to introduce yourself to others. Even if you only get their name at first, you can see them later on campus and have a chat or a meal. Obviously some of the first friends you may meet are in your dorm, perhaps your roommate.

Though everyone is open and friendly at the beginning, often they rapidly fall into cliques or arrangements based on hometowns, class status, posers to class status, those who like to get drunk/high, people who want to act like they're hard, etc. I would advise that you don't try to fall into a small clique too early. You should make good friends—maybe your best friends—but don't shut everyone else out after meeting three or four cool folks. College is about much more than that and you should open yourself to meeting new people, especially those different than yourself.

How many friends should you have? That's a personal decision. My own personal preference is that it's best to have fewer tight friends rather than try to please everyone. I didn't fall into a clique since I was happy to hang out with other people, and my best friends did the same. You don't have to be a social butterfly all the time, and it's important to value time you have alone.

More important than the quantity of friends you have is their quality. If you remember few other things from this book, remember this: your peer group can determine your destiny. Though you may see yourself as an individual, choosing unwisely who you hang out with can have adverse consequences. If none of your friends value studying, do you think this won't affect your study habits? Yeah, you still may go to study but when they say, "I'm not studying for that" about a test, will you laugh and agree? If they smoke pot or do drugs all the time, do you think you'll hang out and not start puffing joints? If they only care about getting drunk and hooking up with chicks, how will you develop your social life?

On the flip side, if they value academics and have a drive to succeed it can definitely help encourage you. If everyone is focused on a higher goal like med school, law school, or just making a difference you can cross-pollinate ideas and give one another crucial support that will improve you all[1]. Also, if they make generally good decisions on a sound moral basis, it will encourage you to do the same. The Booker T. Washington quote at the beginning of this chapter is very apt: if you can't find a good peer group, you are much better off being a loner.

So once you have good friends, does it matter what color they are? In other words, should you only hang with Black people? In my opinion, there are two extremes. Unless you are at an HBCU, there should be no reason why all your friends have to be Black. Even at an HBCU, there are often many students of different races or countries. You are unnecessarily making your life and connections shallower by insisting solely on monoracial friends for reasons that are likely uninformed or even specious.

On the other hand, avoiding Black people or acting "better than thou" for a reason of discomfort or some faux cosmopolitanism has never sat well with me. You don't have to like all Black people and you won't, but that doesn't mean you should have discomfort and be unable to deal with

---

[1] A great example of this is given in the book *The Pact: Three Young Men Make a Promise and Fulfill a Dream* by Sampson Davis, George Jenkins, and Rameck Hunt

them. If you want to learn how to associate with all people, why should Blacks be an exception?

Again there is no rule about how many people of different races or ethnic backgrounds should be in your peer group, but I would suggest you open to them and treat them just as well as you would anyone else. If you came from a predominantly Black neighborhood, this may be the first time you've befriended someone of a different race, and it's best to shelve your preconceptions and treat them as an individual, even if your family has said things about "those people." Their family may have had similar disparaging attitudes toward Blacks for all you know, so if they give you a chance, why not give them one? As with all friends, treat them fairly and as part of your group. If you are going to a party, even if it's predominantly Black, invite them and allow them to decline if they don't want to go. They may be curious and if it's a party open to the public it can't hurt. If they want to talk to a Black girl, don't pull the rug from under them and act shady. They may back you up in the reverse situation later. On the other hand, don't put them in compromising situations if you think there will be issues from others. If they do end up in one of these, have their back like any other friend and try to diffuse the situation.

This may be the first time in the United States for international students. You could be a great help by showing them the ropes and being a touch board for advice. You could also learn a great deal about their country, which could show many of your preconceptions were totally off. They also may be great guides if you can ever visit their country. Often, I saw this ignorance was starkest towards African students. Luckily, growing up I had a family and teachers who taught me real things about Africa, past and present, so I at least knew the countries on the continent, major leaders, and most of the basic issues. Therefore, I didn't make a fool out of myself asking stupid things like if a student from Ghana had elephants in his back-yard—in Accra, in West Africa.

Also, I've found some Black American, West Indian, or African students have a disturbing sense of superiority vis-à-vis one another. I've never figured out the full reason for this, but it's ridiculous and I would encourage you to jettison such feelings and get to know African students as well as about Africa.

Also, don't refuse to try to get to know a person because their group supposedly hates Blacks. Depending on where we come from, there are frictions with Whites, Hispanics, Koreans, Arabs, or someone else. Don't let this be a bar to getting to know someone. Again, they may be much cooler than you can imagine and may be curious about Black people and culture but never had anyone to ask. If they do ask something silly or naïve, don't blow up about it. Just try to make it a positive experience and explain your viewpoint. It is better to gain allies than enemies.

Another group it pays to know is upperclassmen. They know the ropes and can be a valuable source of knowledge and mentoring. Why reinvent the wheel if someone else can tell you how things work? They may have their own peer group but you can still hang with them or start a relationship that can last a lifetime. Having a good upperclass mentor can help you beat the stress, stay in school, and not repeat their mistakes. They can also help provide support or promotion in many important organizations like student government.

Beyond these will be the scores of casual acquaintances you will have across campus or even off campus. There are as many ways to deal with these types of relationships as there are people. Some you may hang out with once every couple of months or only say hi in passing. In general, be respectful and honest. Don't try to front and act like you don't know someone when they pass by. Say hi or nod. It doesn't obligate you to anything. If they are condescending to you, just ignore them from there on out. You should not waste your life trying to please others, but this doesn't give you the right to be hurtful. Yasser Arafat, though controversial as head of the Palestinian Liberation Organization (PLO), had a good quote on friendship: "choose your friends carefully, your enemies will choose you." This is something to always remember in college and beyond.

Romantic and sexual relationships

Okay, some of you are going to think this is the best part of the book. There is not a straight male on the planet who will not admit that one of the best things about college is the size and diversity of its female population. Though this book may have sounded straight-laced for most of its chapters, I want to be completely clear about my intentions here: I strongly encourage you to seek out and engage the ladies at your school. But do so responsibly and intelligently. Let me explain.

Most guys have this vast mental image of college as being the land of milk and honey when it comes to women. It's a great place and relation-ships—or at least casual dating—should definitely be a part of your college experience. Just make sure there's balance. Remember, unless they're rich or insane, your parents aren't paying up to $50,000 a year just for you to chase women.

One of the first things you see up front is the massive difference in many aspects of the female population of college versus high school. First, there are more of them. Second, there is likely a more diverse range of attitudes, body types, looks, etc. I think you can always argue that college girls are prettier since you have more people from a wider geographical area so you get a lot of winners. Also, depending on what college you go to, you may have women from an overall higher economic background than your high school so they can af-ford the clothes, makeup, etc. to accentuate their looks. This is enough to drive the average male in-sane.

As a freshman, dating can be a bit more diffi-cult at times since you are at the bottom of the to-tem pole. The freshman women have a choice of you as well as many upperclassmen. It isn't some-thing that should get you down or be a major ob-stacle, but it can be frustrating. Typical attitudes of freshman men can be extreme. There are the ultra-shy types who are unsure of how to talk to women and don't have confidence. On the other end are the horndogs who see a battlefield and won't wait to make conquests. Others have idealizations of love and are holding out for "the one" and refuse to date anyone else. Most people fall in the moderate ranges, though it can depend a lot on how much you experienced in high school.

How do you handle this?

First of all, there are levels of relationships with women. Some are like the ones in the previous section—friends and acquaintances. However, with women you can go much farther (and make life more complicated). There can be casual dating, serious dating and relationships; there can also be jump-offs and one-night stands. On the more serious side some people find their life partner and get married sooner or later.

However, these relationships typically don't just happen. You have to take initiative and also think about where you want to be at this time in your life. Granted, sometimes love happens despite you making other plans, however, it will pay dividends to at least know how to navigate the dating scene and build from there. Like I've said many times before, this book is not a comprehensive manual on any of its aspects so this chapter is not a how-to guide on bagging women. By posing the typical situations and choices though we can give you a place to start your considerations.

One of the most basic things you should realize before you start dating is that the community of women in a school is what social scientists call a small-world network. This is essentially the idea of six degrees of separation, first popularized by sociologist Stanley Milgram where there are only six associates between any two people in the United States. In college, it is probably two or three degrees of separation. Why is this important? Before you read some book about how to get with women you should realize that you want to make sure you can maximize your dating prospects throughout college and realizing that many women know each other—and talk—is important.

Especially in the Black community, bad behavior by you on dates or with women can rapidly spread and sour your prospects. One of the worst things you can do for your dating prospects is to establish a bad reputation early on in your college career. For example, sometimes women keep lists—yes physical lists—of men who have a reputation for being dogs. Granted, I'm not sure of the exact definition that's always used but typically doing things like dating two girls at once (not casual dates but steady dating), being a player, being abusive, etc. will land you in this category. You don't want to start out your four years by having this type of reputation. I state this upfront since often people come to college with the attitude anything goes without consequence. So your dreams of living the playa lifestyle can be brutally cut short.

Women can often get into the same trouble that guys do when they get labeled players if they put themselves out there too early. There are women I have known that sadly, I knew nothing more about them than the fact that many guys said they were good at something, usually sexual. That label stuck even though I had absolutely no idea how true it was. There is a double standard for guys in this aspect as far as behavior, but you still must remember that your reputation matters and you can only sell your integrity once. On the other hand I wouldn't be honest if I didn't mention there are girls who are also down with that type of lifestyle and being a playa may help you in those circles. Just realize that these are usually not the types that want more than a good night so if you are looking for relationship material, don't live life to the contrary.

College is one of the best and easiest times in your life to date. You will possibly never see another time with such a deep pool of potential partners with such an ease of access. Therefore, college is a great time to perfect your skills at dealing with the opposite sex. First, you need to get over the barrier of talking to girls if that's still an issue for you. Girls aren't supernatural beings. They actually probably have more insecurities than you ever do, so there's no reason to lack confidence. The best thing is not to act like something you aren't. Don't parrot some mack you saw someone else do or got from a movie. Every girl responds to different things, and you need to perfect your own groove. Also, you need to learn to not take rejection personally. A lot of the guys who seem to have girls all the time realized early on dating is a numbers game. If two-thirds of girls tell you no but you talk to nine, that's three girls you have succeeded with. It's not the end of the world if some girl you have obsessed over pays you no heed. There are too many fish in the sea.

I knew guys who had never asked a girl for her phone number before. Working yourself up to get beyond these psychological barriers is key because otherwise, there are likely no first dates. Also, sending emails, giving someone a business card, or giving a woman your phone number are usually game enders. Women usually want men to take some initiative and those actions make it seem like you have none.

Once you get past all this you can go on dates. Dating can be fun or nerve-racking depending on how you handle it. In college, you should definitely date and realize many things about dating. I can't list them all here but here are some top ones. First, casual dating is not serious. If you are not in a steady relationship, you should be open and available to talk to or even date other women. If there is a problem with this from one of the girls they obviously have different expectations than you and you should deal with this accordingly, depending on what you want.

Second, dating does not have to be expensive or elaborate. Of course dinner and movies are the most common themes, but the same restaurant can get boring and expensive pretty quickly. Being creative and open minded is key here, and there are often cheaper options such as art or science museums, plays from university or other theater groups, jazz or classical music concerts, or even cooking classes that can give a great time without breaking one's budget. In addition, you can learn a lot about someone by the types of activities they appreciate. If they disdain anything but the mundane and aren't open to new experiences they may be shallower than you originally thought. If they demand you go to expensive restaurants or financially strain yourself they may be higher maintenance than it's worth. It's up to you what you'll tolerate.

Third, dating is fake, especially in the beginning. If you have a few good first dates and you think you know the person or know she's "the one," don't be completely won over. The important stuff, such as the things that get on your nerves, typically only come out later as the relationship evolves. Finally, don't forget chivalry and romance.

No matter what women say about being modern, liberated, etc., they all appreciate someone who opens the door, pulls out their chair for them and is attentive enough to do sweet things like bringing them flowers or writing love letters. Yes, I said love letters—with pen and paper, not Facebook. Conversely, never use derogatory words like bitch or ho, which are never fit to be directed at anyone, no matter their actions. Romance has faded a bit, which makes it much more valuable to someone who appreciates its power.

One thing you will have to decide when you date is how early you want to be locked into a serious relationship. I have friends who met their spouse the first week of college and others who never had a serious relationship in college. Again, love happens and is not always predictable, but being new to college I would advise you to be circumspect at first. You don't have to get seriously involved with the first girl you date if you don't want to, and it may be to your benefit to test the waters or just hang out until you are ready for something more serious. There are a lot of people in college, and sometimes it's best to sit back and observe for a bit to see what they're like before doing anything serious. Granted, the down side is they may be scooped by someone else in the meantime, but don't fall into the trap of grabbing the first girl you meet. This will have the effect of limiting your options just when they are starting to expand. Often the ones most noticed tend to be the most social and perhaps "easiest" while the true gems may be more worried about hitting the books than dressing to kill.

One of the best ways to meet cool women is to not try to fight every other guy for the same dime piece everyone is talking about. She may not even be worth it anyway. Keep your eyes and options open so you will be able to figure out what you really want. Doing this you will discover there are many different types of girls in college that fit almost all categories of description.

You will eventually find out who is nice and who is mean, who is intense and who is relaxed, who is reserved and who sleeps around, etc. Never make the mistake of correlating two qualities that may seem to be mutually interdependent but are not. For example, book smarts and common sense. I have seen very intelligent women make some of the dumbest decisions when it comes to men and relationships. The same goes for social class and behavior. Don't assume that someone will act a certain way because they have a certain background be it poor, rich, private school, or public school. There are some girls who act like little angels in public and then get down with the grimiest dude on campus behind closed doors. Be careful what you assume about someone from their public front.

No matter what kind of people you run into though, it is important to never lose the basic respect you should have toward women. Often people get jaded by relationships or past failures and denigrate all women as a result. There is never a need for this, and it reflects more on your shallow ego than the actual state of things. If you give up on women, of course they will all seem bad since your actions toward them will help generate a self-fulfilling prophecy. If it ever seems too much, just take a break. They aren't going anywhere.

If you do get into a long-term relationship, make sure you keep it healthy and help each other grow. There is no reason a healthy relationship should cause you to neglect your grades or isolate you from your friends or campus life. It's fine that she's the apple of your eye, but it's not healthy for your world to begin and end solely with her. If you have nothing else but the relationship, a breakup could be all the more devastating. In addition, if you decide to enter a relationship, realize what it is: exclusive. If you have the urge to cheat or sow your oats, *don't get into a committed relationship*. You aren't ready for it and I would argue that this is just fine. There's nothing wrong with someone who doesn't want to settle for just one person. You're young and that isn't necessarily want you want or need at this time. There should be no reason to cheat on someone or creep on your girlfriend if you're in a relationship for the right reasons. If you can't hold to this, break up no matter how much the initial pain is.

The most important thing for any relationship is communication. There's no aspect of your relationship that open communication cannot enhance. Lack of communication is what destroys many relationships. If you can't trust her enough to discuss issues openly, it speaks volumes about your relationship and whether it should be long-term. Also, don't make your relationship gossip. If you have an issue with your girlfriend, take it up with her or with friends in confidence. Don't put your business in the street. In addition, don't let others tell you what you should be doing or where you should be going with your relationship. Whatever decisions you make, you will be the one to deal with it, not the peanut gallery.

Characteristics of a good relationship

What is a good relationship? This is another question you could literally write books on. A good relationship can also mean many things to many people depending on where you are in life, where you are going, and what you want at the time. If you're looking for jump-offs, a good relationship to you may be a low drama, easy in/out, friends with benefits situation. If you are looking for a life partner it can mean someone who is low-key, shares your values, and has your back no matter what.

There are several characteristics that stretch across functional, committed relationships.

1. Open communication—As stated above, the bottom line is if you can't communicate openly and without fear of drama with your girl, your relationship will be rocky and in danger of failure. Communication is the glue that binds relationships not because it prevents conflict but because relationships are often about conflict. Many people have false, fairy tale dreams of love that think it is an absence of friction in the relationship. True love is not a lack of friction but the presence of the lubrication that prevents the friction from burning you two out. If you can communicate, conflicts may come and go but they will get resolved. If you can't, the pressure builds until something blows up. Some people can have long-term relationships that are defined by frequent and vociferous fights, but what way is that to

live? If you cannot express your hopes, fears, reservations, and disagreements with someone you love, you really need to improve this part of your relationship. One final note on modern communication: Facebook, Twitter, and texting are not mediums of communication in a relationship. They can be good to check on someone, say hi, or plan things, but it's a mark of laziness to rely on them to communicate with your significant other. Don't make it your primary mode of communication if you expect to keep the girl and make her happy.

2. Support—I have never understood why some people are in relationships with people who do not support or even sabotage them. You have a lot of problems with haters in life without being with the enemy. You need someone who supports you and your goals but is also willing to give honest feedback. Someone who does not support you, wants to just use you, wants to sabotage you to make you something else, or is jealous of you is not good relationship material.

3. Similar values and goals—When you are initially in love, the values and goals aspect doesn't matter so much. You are head over heels. As time passes though, the values of a person will affect their decisions and ultimately impact the relationship. Do you share similar values regarding trust, male/female roles, education, your identity as a Black person, religion, etc.? You do not

have to have identical ideals, but if they seriously clash it will show up sooner or later. Ideals are touchy and not always a deal breaker but you should face up to them and realize that if this is going to be long-term, your values will need to have some alignment.

4. Financial trust—Can you trust her with money? Not just if she spends money every now and then on things she wants, but is she a financial wreckage? Is she getting you to pay her credit card bills, other bills, or cannot exercise any responsible spending? If this describes her, be careful! Money destroys many relationships and marriages and can be a very sore subject. If you cannot trust her to spend her own money wisely, she'll eventually spend your money unwisely.

5. Sexual compatibility—Well, the next section is about sex but I will be real here. If you go down the path of sex, long-term relationships and marriages do demand sexual compatibility. If someone isn't enjoying it or has different ideas about what and how much they need, this could become a huge drag on the relationship.

6. Similar ideas about relationships—You need to make sure you both have the same idea about relationships. This is similar to values. If she sees relationships as mutual and reciprocal, you're a lucky man. If she feels she should be a parasite and you're the

latest host, you better recognize and move on. Relationships should never be a one-way street.

Sex

This chapter is about relationships, but let's not kid each other about what many modern relationships entail: sex. In today's age, it's not even necessary to have a traditional relationship to be sexually active, so unsurprisingly sex dominates a lot of the discussions of relationships on college campuses. Sex is the most intimate expression possible between a man and a woman, even if it only means you're just horny. Sex is natural, and I'm not about to tell you when to have sex or definitely not how to have sex. What I can do is make sure you have everything in context.

Sex is great, otherwise so many people would not do stupid things, ruin relationships, or even ruin lives to get it. On the other hand, when you let the wrong head control your life you can court disaster. If there is anything in history that has destroyed men who otherwise are intelligent about everything else, lust would rank with greed as a top contender. Again, I am not saying these things to make sex seem bad, just remember there is a moral and safety aspect to everything you do and sex is no exception. You don't have to write sex out of your life, but if you do it you need to realize there are steps to take to make sure it's more likely to be a positive experience.

First, always use protection. No excuses. Your own protection, by which I mean a condom you've brought yourself. The threat of pregnancies and sexually transmitted diseases is too great for you to rely on anyone else to provide protection for you. This will be discussed more in the health and safety section, but there's a reason why people get pregnant and that STDs are rampant. No good feeling from even a marathon sex session is worth it if it means you're stuck with a disease or baby. If you don't take your own responsibility for birth control ("but she's on the pill"), you can only blame yourself if things don't go well. This is too crucial a time in your life to derail yourself, so it's best to play it safe. There are lots of brands of condoms—all sizes, thicknesses, and materials—out these days. You can find something that works. Be sure you also look up how to carry around condoms in a manner that won't damage or degrade them (hint: not your wallet). That way they will be available in even unexpected situations.

You may not set out to go to some girl's room to do anything but study or watch a movie but you start cuddling, then making out, and before you know it you're in bed. Always be prepared since when your hormones take over many people don't know how to stop. Do you think anyone plans an unwanted pregnancy? If you do end up in an intimate situation, stay safe. Afterward, treat the lady with some respect. Don't just give her a kiss and bounce. Treat her like someone of worth and go to breakfast or at least compliment her. Women are a lot more emotional than men and so a small disrespect you may think of as nothing could be interpreted as a major slight.

Again, as in relationships, don't put your business in the street. Guys are competitive, and many times the first thing we want to do is run and tell our boys and talk about how you're the man. Don't drop all the lurid details out there. First, many women value their reputation, and regardless of what you just did, they don't want it ruined. Second, if you're sleeping around to get validation from your peers you're in the wrong peer group.

Really, peer validation shouldn't be your goal. Don't get in a competition to get notches and end up treating women and their feelings like points in a game. Hell hath no fury like a woman scorned, and things can come around and bite you hard if you aren't careful.

There's a lot of talk on campuses nowadays about the "hookup culture" and how it's replacing dating. It isn't really that new since it was in college when I was there as well. So jump-offs are becoming the substitutes for girlfriends? It's pretty tempting as a guy. If chicks are living like Carrie on *Sex and the City*, why bother with all the relationship crap? This seems especially cogent in recent years where women are now outnumbering men on most major college campuses that aren't engineering schools. Cut all the flowers and chocolates and whip out the Trojan. Again, whatever you do is your decision, but I still want to emphasize if you ever want a real relationship you're going to have to practice the finer social skills of courtship. You can run around for four years straight but don't act like you're going to go from that to a committed relationship with "the one" without any difficulties. I'm not going to tell you the kind of life you should want, but don't act like any given decision doesn't have consequences.

Sex is a complex topic. To delve completely into even its superficial aspects is out of the scope of this book, and there are entire sections at bookstores you can look at to get the down and dirty details. Just remember that sex is best always as a means and never as an end in relationships. Also remember the old saying, "women give sex for love and men give love for sex."

Interracial relationships

Thirty years ago, interracial relationships were so rare that they were a matter of intense discussion on many college campuses. In fact, before the 1970s the lower their income and education, Blacks were more likely to interracially marry and poorer people in rural areas were more likely to marry outside their race. Now the likelihood has flipped and higher education and income are a positive correlating factor with dating and marrying outside one's race.

Interracial relationships are pretty common these days though by common I mean only in certain combinations. You are much, much more likely to see a White man with an Asian woman than an Asian man with a Black woman. The former probably wouldn't turn heads, the latter would invite stares. In addition, interracial relationships are more accepted on some campuses than others. There is no set rule on how every campus responds to interracial couples, but it can depend on how relatively liberal the views on race are there, how cosmopolitan the student body is, and which kind of couples are tolerated. Again places where it is accepted for Whites to date Asians or Hispanics for example may not be as open to Whites dating Blacks or Blacks dating Asians. Every place can have its own weird logic.

As an established fact, Black men date and marry outside their race at a greater frequency than Black women do. This is consistent across all parts of the United States and even different countries such as the United Kingdom and Canada though their rates of Black interracial marriage for both sexes are multiples of the rate in the U.S. The rates of interracial dating for both Black men and women have grown with time, so there's a high likelihood that a Black male going to a non-HBCU could be in an interracial relationship.

At the core, these relationships are just like any other, especially if she grew up in the United States, regardless of her race. It's more likely that things like religion will cause friction than the fact that you are from different ethnic groups. There are unique issues that impinge upon interracial relationships from both the outside world and the Black community.

There are still people who don't accept Black men dating outside their race. These can be both non-Blacks and Blacks. Some may keep this to themselves while others may be more assertive such as stares, trying to sabotage you, or causing other issues. Physical attacks and verbal insults are much rarer now than they once were but still happen on occasion. People will also try to impugn your reasons for being in a relationship suggesting for example that you want something easy or "you can't handle a Black woman."

There can also be family and culture issues. Straight up, some families or ethnic groups have low or no tolerance for their daughters dating and especially marrying Black men. Sometimes, you may have to deal with the fact that she cannot tell her family about you or if she does, they may communicate complete disapproval to the point of trying to break up the relationship. You would think this would be outdated in the 21st century but it's not. It may not matter if you come from a good two-parent home, have a good education, and have high aspirations. They may not get past the "he's Black" aspect.

You can definitely work with your girl to win them over, and this may take commitment. Sometimes, this commitment can bring you both closer and make the relationship better. Other times it can tear you apart. If this is your situation you should gauge how much you're willing to fight for love. Love conquers all but any conquest has a price. Your partner has to have your back 100%. If she doesn't stand up for you, there may be a serious question if the relationship can work. You should also know what their expectations are since some people come from backgrounds where they want to get married early and settle down. If that's her goal, then you should be down or be out.

On the other hand, her family may be neutral or even adore you, which is a great situation. That makes the relationship much easier to manage and allows the bigger issues of any relationship to take precedence. No matter what though, you'll have to deal with others.

First, whatever your reasons are for being in any relationship, you don't have to prove yourself or seek approval from anyone. If they don't accept you for your choice, why is that your problem? Second, if you need to explain or defend yourself, refer to this being your choice and emphasize the best aspects about your girlfriend. Talk about the positive aspects of the relationship, the fact that it's your life and your choice, and in the end, it is not anyone else's business. Don't be overly hostile or defensive—just be plain and try to make them see the other person for who they are, beyond their race.

In my opinion, there can be distasteful or even wrong ways to defend an interracial relationship. One of the most distasteful defensive reactions to unjustified scrutiny is putting down other Blacks or the Black community in general. Often, there are some Black men who will focus on how negative Black women supposedly are in some aspect, be this from their personal experience or just a viewpoint. First, though you have a right to not prefer Black women, you do not have the right to pass a blanket dismissal or insult upon them. Trust me, if you think you can stereotype Black women, you've been dating from too shallow of a pool, possibly by your own fault. Second, how do you think your partner would feel if she believed you liked her because you're running away from something else or are insecure about being Black? I've always believed this is a wrong way to go about defending your choice, even if society at large or the members of the Black community are unjustly maligning you.

Breakups

Unless you meet and marry your first love, which can happen, you'll have to deal with a breakup. Even if you marry your first love, there's a high probability you'll break up and get back together at least once. In fact, this can be a healthy part of learning about relationships. Breakups are never cool and few people want to be on the receiving end. Even if you want to end a relationship for good reasons, the process can be very emotionally painful.

Breakups happen, however, and it's best to learn to deal with them from both the dishing and receiving end. They're never easy, and it'll come down to a decision of the ethics of commitment versus a desire to leave a relationship. A lot of magazines and pop psychology say the decision is "easy"—that if you don't feel in super-love, heart a-flutter all the time then you should just break up. True, if you don't like a relationship and especially if it's dangerous or abusive you should end it. However, there's a balance between the ethics of commitment and doing what's easy. If you don't want to take the "next step" with someone, it's a valid reason to end a relationship because you both aren't looking in the same direction. On the other hand, just because you had a fight or a bad day doesn't mean you just can't be together. Like the weather, no long-term relationship is all about happy, sunny days. If you truly feel dedicated to a person and love them, troubles are something you can work to overcome, not use as a convenient excuse to bail.

But there are times when you two just weren't meant to be, and you will likely experience them. First, if you are thinking constantly about breaking up with someone, there's something wrong in the relationship. You should discuss it amongst yourselves and analyze it, but if it cannot be changed by either person's actions, it's better to break it off sooner rather than later. Yes, you will hurt the person's feelings and she will likely cry. You may feel like an asshole and some people will question your logic in ditching such a "great" person, but at the end of the day, you and not the social gossipers, will have to live with this person, and if you can't do it, screw the peanut gallery and end it.

In my experience, the direct and personal approach is best. First, do the breakup in person. If you break up over text or worse in a public forum like Facebook or Twitter, you are an idiot and an ass, period. No matter how terrible you think she is, every woman deserves a minimal amount of respect and if you are a real man you won't be afraid to confront her in person. Second, don't do stupid stuff like spending the night and hang out with the girl before breaking up with her. Just do it. I can't tell you how because I'm not sure there's any art to something like this. But be honest and don't insult her intelligence with "it's not you it's me" crap. Also, don't be cruel, especially in something this emotionally searing. No matter what you say or do though, it's going to be bad so don't judge yourself by the level of her emotional outbursts. Be honest, don't be cruel, do it, then just leave.

On the other hand, you may get dumped. Hopefully she will do it tactfully. Similar rules apply here but first, do not let rage or anger get the better of you, and never issue any threats or physical violence. Don't do anything you'll regret later and though you may be tempted, don't plot revenge. It's not worth it and will usually backfire. In this situation, and even where you initiate the breakup, it can often help to talk to friends, male or female, for consolation, help, and advice. If the friend is female, don't use her for sympathy sex. You probably need to take a break from women for a little bit and get yourself back together.

Post-breakup, it can be emotionally precarious. First, don't ever let your sadness force you into mental breakdown or suicidal thoughts. You're not the first, or the last, to experience this and to be honest, there are many more women out there. When I was ever in this situation I would listen to a few good oldies like "Too Many Fish in the Sea" by the Marvalettes or "Rainbow" by Gene Chandler. They help put things in perspective. One thing you definitely don't want is for this to impact your schoolwork or health. You must maintain. You can feel bad, keep to yourself, be alone, cry, or cope however you want but don't damage your future over this. Wrecking your health or grades will cause you a pain that will last long after you get over the girl.

Use your friends as support. Don't clam up and keep it all inside. Even if you trust only one person, talk to them. If you need help, ask for it. That's what real friends are for. In the end, relationships come and go, but you're stuck with yourself. Don't let someone else destroy you and your future.

Relationships and schoolwork

Taking a cue from the last section, we should discuss relationships and schoolwork. I could tell stories for hours about friends who didn't go to med school, dropped out, or otherwise damaged themselves academically over relationship issues. This can range from being madly in love, playing the field, suffering from a bad breakup, or getting a girl pregnant.

Relationships should complement your time at school, not impede it. If you're in a relationship that's interfering with your schoolwork, you need to fix the relationship or end it. Trust me, if you drop out or hurt your future prospects, that girl may be gone anyway. Touching on values again, if a girl doesn't value your academic success and well-being more than her desire to party or get attention, she's bad news. She may not make it and will drag you down with her.

Girlfriends can be excellent study partners but you should do this in moderation for several reasons. First, studying with your girl can be a distraction as you flirt and talk when you should study. Second, being in a relationship already monopolizes your time to a certain extent to the point that you may become socially isolated because of it. If you even study with her it may leave little time to know or interact with others. She isn't going anywhere. Study with other friends or those in your classes, and don't become a whipped social hermit.

Relationship safety

Relationships can be dangerous. Though men are much less at risk for physical abuse than women, the dangers can still exist. We already discussed emotional abuse some earlier. There can be much more dangerous things and people, however.

Crazy Girls/Stalkers

Some women are just crazy. Some guys like this because it's exciting—they're uninhibited and freaky, etc. But eventually the craziness goes bad. By crazy I mean someone with a continuous, severe mental imbalance that can include violent mood swings, bizarre behavior, uncontrolled anger or emotional outbursts, and threatening behavior like stalking. I'm of the opinion that messing with crazy girls is eventually a losing proposition. The breakup itself could put you through an ordeal, so it's better to be circumspect. Sometimes the craziness doesn't show until later since people can hide their true selves on dates. Granted, I can agree that many average women have crazy moments or times, but if it's a consistent, overriding feature of her personality, she may be nuts.

No one should make you fear for your safety. In addition, no one should engage in threatening behavior like stalking and harassment, which is now unfortunately easier due to cyberspace and social networking. Stalkers are no fun and are typically indicative of someone who is at least slightly nuts. If someone is harassing you and has ignored repeated calls to desist, it could merit a call to campus security. Sadly many people don't back off unless told to by the law.

Likewise, you should not stalk anyone. This includes calling repeatedly, following them on social media, or tracking them. If they don't want you, move on.

Rape

One of the biggest crimes you can commit short of murdering someone is rape. It also carries one of the greatest stigmas. There are many men who purposely or even inadvertently commit sexual assault on campuses everywhere. An act that may seem innocuous at the time can eventually lead to an accusation, arrest, discipline, and imprisonment. This can be a relationship safety issue for men as well as women, not because men are as likely to get raped, but that the typical campus rapist is not some cold, oversexed predator but often someone who allows himself to get out of hand.

I know this sounds clichéd, but never force someone into sex if they don't want to have it. If they say no, just don't do it. I know that some women play hard to get or that you often have to be assertive as a man, but there should be no illusion that doing the deed will loosen her up. If they don't want to do it and won't close the deal, just stop. If the cops are called later, what will you say, "she really wanted it?"

First, one of the biggest contributors to date rape is being under the influence of drugs or alcohol. Being drunk lowers your inhibitions and can make it much likelier that you'll take things further than they should go. This can be even easier if it's with a relative stranger. It's also easier because if the woman is drunk or high, her inhibitions can be near zero.

It also affects both memories. The shame and shock of waking up from having had sex, especially unprotected, can cause a girl to wonder if she was raped and lead to an accusation. I'm not implying these accusations are not genuine, but these types of situations can be very risky and being drunk or especially high is no defense. To be safe, I would say only get it on if you're in your right mind or relatively sober. The only exception could be a long-term relationship, but just remember situations with alcohol, drugs, and sex can and often do end badly. Under absolutely no circumstances should you actively get someone drunk or high, especially if they're under drinking age, in order to make them easier.

If you're accused of rape and the victim is someone underage you helped get drunk, you're in a world of trouble. In any case, what does it say about your game if you have to get a girl drunk to look at you?

Conflicts over women

As men, we can be aggressive about what we want, and some guys start beef or get in fights over women. I've never seen this be worth it unless you're defending yourself and your girl. First, it proves nothing. The girl has made up her mind, and if she's going to change it because of a fight she's the type of flake you should avoid. Second, some idiots come back with knives or guns and make the argument a fatal encounter. A close friend of mine had a friend die over something like this in a fight at a party. Not worth it. Finally, if you start messing with someone else's girl— something else I don't recommend—tell her to make a decision: she has to stay with her man or leave him. Don't play around with someone who won't leave a relationship they're in. She wants to have her cake and eat it too.

Relationships with faculty and administrators

Now that romance is out of the way, we can talk about a few more types of important relationships. Some important but often neglected relationships are those with school faculty and administrators. Your most common interaction will be with faculty such as your professors. Further up the chain are department chairs, deans, or even college presidents and rectors.

Professors have a special emphasis as your most common encounter. Always respect professors, especially in class. I only made the mistake

131

once of making an unintentionally disrespectful comment in class, and I'm thankful I didn't get flunked. Some people are intentionally challenging or disrespectful. Even if your professor says something you profoundly disagree with, you must meet him or her on their own turf with a respectful, yet reasoned and forceful argument. Don't try to humiliate or diminish them in the eyes of your classmates or their peers. Professors control your grades and also have a wealth of contacts and opportunities.

If you participate frequently in class, it makes it easier for a professor to respect your opinion than if you just talk once a semester, so stay engaged. You should always go to every professor's office hours at least twice a semester. This is where they get to put a face and a personality to your name. It's also where you can get help and tips on upcoming assignments or tests. If you have a serious problem with a professor, it's also better to bring it up in office hours rather than trying to blow up the lecture. It gives you both a chance to talk through it without the fear of backing down that often accompanies arguments in front of large groups.

Professors may also offer after-hours meetups that are not required by the class. I encourage you to attend these and get to know the professors and other students. This could also lead to more opportunities such as mentoring. Professors, especially those in areas in which you have an interest, can be great mentors both on formal projects and in larger career pursuits. You should try to find at least one mentor among the faculty after at least a year on campus. This will help you make better career choices, navigate the university easier, and avoid many common mistakes. They can also be a great way to find out about promising research opportunities, if that's what's up your alley.

If the class has a TA, this relationship can also be important as mentioned in the chapter on academics. Going to the problem sessions and even TA hours can help you build a good relationship and even obtain help.

A bit higher in the hierarchy are administrators. These people usually come into contact with students due to students' involvement with some kind of special extracurricular activity or award. These relationships can be very valuable and open many opportunities. Meeting administrators though requires more polish than professors. For first meetings wear collared shirts and slacks, not jeans or flip-flops. Act polished and treat the administrator with respect. In addition, understand their time is extremely valuable, and be careful not to waste it. Before you meet, go to the school website and look up their name and position to understand what they do so you don't seem totally ignorant.

For higher level administrators like presidents or board members, wearing a suit and tie is a good idea. You should also ask other faculty or administrators you know how to behave. Don't talk too much but answer questions clearly and intelligently. Don't use slang or vernacular, but don't be overly stuffy either. Relax and be yourself—false pretense always reeks.

One last resource is the Office of Black Affairs, or whatever it is called on your campus. I have always been puzzled about how few Black students take advantage of the resources and programs the Office of Black Affairs offers. The office emerged from the battles of the 1960s to help Black students succeed, and it often goes underutilized. This should be one of your first few stops on campus to familiarize yourself with the people and opportunities it offers. Some such as community events, tutoring, or even research opportunities can be well worth it. The deans can also give you the inside knowledge of campus politics and events, which can be essential.

Your reputation

As important as your relationships is your reputation. That's the general view in which you are held that touches on your personality, morality, and past actions. As previously stated, you can only sell your integrity once, and this is very true. Maintaining your integrity is one of the most important facets of keeping your relationships healthy. That means not lying to friends, lovers, or faculty and making good decisions. Your reputation travels much faster than you think, and people sadly more remember your ills and mistakes than your successes.

On the other hand, never compromise your own personal beliefs for a good social reputation. If you are going to have to betray someone or your ideals to make others happy, it is usually not worth it. Even in this situation, your reputation as someone who stands for something and is independent can hold you in good stead, even with your enemies. Keep your head high and do the right thing and you'll see your reputation create opportunities for you.

A final thing you can do to build character is working on important character skills, some of which was mentioned in the chapter on academics including public speaking and etiquette. Other useful skills are learning how to taste and identify wines and tying neckties (there are more than just the most common knots). Finally, you should learn how to network. This will be discussed more in Chapter 11, but is definitely a worthwhile skill to build character.

Conclusion

Relationships are an essential part of college life and can make or break your experience just as much as grades can. Though these tips are only a start, hopefully they can help guide you to make good decisions and have the best college experience possible.

Chapter 5
Health and Safety

There are always relationships and interactions between physical and mental health... the mind-body connection is ever present, but the mental health component often receives secondary attention or no attention at all... If you don't value your own life, you neglect your health. If you don't value your own life, you're more likely to engage in risky behaviors. If you don't value your own life, you lose motivation to succeed.
—Dr. Alvin F. Poussaint

Health and safety are of the utmost importance in college. Of course, everyone wants to stay healthy and safe, but a surprising number of people neglect both in their pursuit of fun, success, sex, or all three. In this chapter we will discuss the basic health and safety issues you'll confront and how to handle them most effectively.

Basic health

A lot of this may seem obvious and even a bit insulting but I just want to cover all the basics. You should shower every day—or at least every two days. You may laugh but I know people who didn't and you could smell it. You should also use deodorant, and if you need it, body powder to control excess perspiration. You'll often leave your dorm early in the morning and return late at night (or the next morning). You need to prepare accordingly.

Included in this is brushing your teeth and flossing. You should floss at least every night. The college diet can wreck your teeth, and flossing is important in keeping them clean. I got a cavity every two years until I started flossing in college and have hardly had one since. You should also shave regularly unless you're going for the grown or shaggy look. If you want the latter, you should keep your hair, beard, and mustache well-kept. Often when you come on campus, representatives of major shaver companies will hand out "free" shaving kits. How nice. Like I said in the finance chapter, nothing is free. The business model of many of these companies is to give away the razors and then once you like it, you'll continue to buy the expensive razor blades. If you like the ordinary razors, these free razors are a great gift. If you're worried about this expense, you may want to consider a good electric razor, which doesn't require replacements of blades frequently.

You also want to get your hair cut obviously. There are usually three main options: a barber, a skilled fellow student, or doing it yourself. Obviously the latter is the cheapest in the long term but can be difficult and you may not get it right for a few tries. As for barbers, you probably want to find a Black barber shop. If there's not one on or near campus, you can find the Black part of town (if there is one) and usually you will find a good shop. If you aren't from the area, you can ask other Black students which shops are best and in the safest areas since some larger cities and even smaller ones can have high crime areas you must be careful around as a non-local even if you're Black.

Before you head to school you need to get a checkup from your personal physician. Make sure you're up to date on all vaccinations. Most of these you probably have for life but some like tetanus may need to be renewed. Given the nature of college I would recommend getting both the hepatitis A and B vaccinations. If you have prescription meds, such as those for asthma, you'll want to go to your doctor and get your prescription filled for college. Also, the typical over-the-counter drugs like painkillers, antacid, and allergy medicine are necessary. It's advisable to pick up a cheap first-aid kit and first-aid cream for accidents. You want to get a dentist appointment, too, to get a good cleaning so you'll have a nice white set of teeth starting school.

One point of health that's often neglected is room cleanliness. Your room doesn't have to be sparkling, but you shouldn't neglect basic rules of sanitation. Have a clothes hamper and put your dirty clothes there—and only there. Wash your sheets at least once every two weeks. Also, don't leave food open or lying in the room since it attracts pests and is generally unsanitary. You should take trash out whenever it's full and not leave it an unseemly mess. Sweeping up every now and then is good as well. Some dorms provide cleaning supplies, otherwise you need to get them yourself.

Same goes for the bathroom. Pick up the washcloths and towels. Every couple of weeks you and your dorm mates need to organize a cleaning unless this is done by university staff. Finally, when leaving for break, make sure you clean out the fridge and remove any ice so there won't be a rotting, wet mess if the fridge fails or the power goes out.

Diet

One of the biggest downfalls of health is the typical undergraduate diet. The 'freshman 15'— fifteen pounds some students add freshman year— is common and quite true. For some who are underweight, this can be okay. For others, it can mean the difference between being in shape and overweight or overweight and obese. The reasons for this are fairly obvious. Not all cafeteria food is healthy. In addition, you'll be staying up much later than in high school and snacking on pizza at 11:00 P.M. can become a common ritual. Combine this with long study hours, reduced exercise, and alcohol consumption, and you are asking for calorie overload.

If you're anything like me, when you go to college you may have never looked at the calories on the back of anything. As a swimmer I worked out so much my eating habits had very little effect on my weight, and I would pound carbs before swim meets for maximum performance. You don't have to go to the extremes of weird diets or starving yourself, but you may want to watch what you eat.

However, the first lesson about college diets is the opposite of what I've mentioned: you should eat three meals a day. For maximum performance and health, you shouldn't skip either breakfast or lunch. By doing this you'll only push off your hunger, worsen your attention span due to low blood sugar, and encourage yourself to overeat at dinner or indulge in small unhealthy snacks like chips and soda throughout the day. Even if you're trying to lose weight, the key is to watch what you eat, not stop eating.

So let's look at a typical day and understand the diet. First off when you wake up is breakfast. Whether your thing is cereal or grits or pancakes, you should get something solid. In addition, you should have a piece of fruit, and maybe some eggs. You can also have meat like bacon in moderation. The key for eating is moderation. If you get pancakes, get two not four. The same applies for sausage, bacon, or anything else. You don't have to pig out and may not want to unless you are an athlete or in ROTC. Oatmeal and grits were my personal favorite and I would usually combine these with fruit like a banana and boiled eggs. Again, moderation applies to both sides of the coin. Don't eat too much but also, don't fool yourself that a bowl of sugary cereal is a substitute for a real breakfast.

If you need to snack, keep something in your bag like a piece of fruit such as an apple, orange, a granola bar, or trail mix to keep you going. This will also help in staying away from fast food restaurants and other quick meals that are bad for you. One big way to keep calories under control is to drink water or coffee (with minimal cream and sugar) instead of sugary drinks like soda.

For lunch, you may often be on the run. Lunch has more options than breakfast, so you can use your meal plan to eat at the cafeteria or go to local restaurants. Another option, to save money or calories, is to make your own lunch. Given most dorms don't have full kitchens, lunch may be the only thing you can make and a sandwich with chips and a piece of fruit like an apple can be just what you need to stay in your calorie budget and get through the day.

For dinner you can typically have a nice meal at the venue of your choice. If you live in an apartment you can cook and the best way to do this with a busy schedule is to fix a large amount of food Sunday evening that can last you through most of the week. That way you can have home-cooked leftovers all week without the hassle of shopping or cooking a new meal. Just remember, the typical dinner has a meat, a starch (i.e. rice or potatoes), and a vegetable. No, pepperoni pizza with peppers and onions does not cover all these. Also, never forget a good woman is always impressed with a man who can cook.

Often you'll be up late at night. If you ate dinner at 6:00 P.M., by 10:00 P.M. or so the munchies may start calling again. Here's where late night snacking can destroy the most meticulously planned meal schedule. Around every campus is an eatery who delivers up until midnight or later. Typically it's not healthy food. It's fine to do this occasionally—I still have a soft spot for ranch dressing on cheese pizza—but if this becomes a habit it will affect your waistline. Stay away from carb heavy and fatty food late at night. You may want to stash some healthier options in your dorm to be on hand if you get hungry.

If you want to understand what your daily caloric intake should be and how to balance a healthy diet, there are a variety of resources you can use. The Mayo Clinic online has a Healthy Lifestyle page that has a calorie counter, dietary recommendations, and other articles on fat, salt, and even energy drinks. The school health clinic will also likely have free literature or even classes on maintaining a healthy diet as a student. Remember weight gain comes from unused calories that you eat and don't burn off during normal activity or exercise. Also, know the difference between saturated fats (typically solid such as butter or red meat) and unsaturated fats (typically liquid vegetable oils) and how you should limit your intake of the former.

Another important part of health is keeping up with vitamins and nutrients. There are some basic vitamins that it could help to take regularly to stay healthy and keep up immunity. This could include vitamin C, vitamin D, calcium, multivitamins, and various other supplements like garlic. Check with a health professional or the school health center to see what's best for you.

Diet is good for more than just keeping your weight in check. Your diet can affect your wider health such as susceptibility to illness. This can work both ways. An unhealthy diet or skipping meals can make you more likely to get sick. I battled my first bout of flu and was out for almost a week my freshman year. Part of me getting sick was that I had been doing a poor job getting meals due to my busy schedule. Don't make the same mistake.

Eating disorders

Don't laugh. I know what you are thinking: This is some chick crap. Dudes don't do the whole anorexia and bulimia weirdness. A man's desired physique is muscle bound and fit, not some bony supermodel ideal. Well, you're wrong and the sad fact is that eating disorders among men do exist. Men comprise about ten percent of all diagnosed eating disorders according to research studies. These can often be the same disorders as women such as anorexia or bulimia with the primary goal being weight loss.

Other times, many men get into extreme diets—often to build muscle mass—that are not nutritionally healthy. These often involve massive intakes of protein with a minimization of carbohydrates, fruits, and vegetables. There are appropriate ways to diet in order to maximize the effectiveness of strength training, but don't believe everything just because you read it in a magazine, book, or on a website. Some of these diets have been developed with only quick results in mind and neglect to focus on short or long-term health effects. If you're wondering what regimen is best and healthiest, the school health clinic or the medical personnel at the athletic department can be a great help. There are special diets that athletes use that are time-tested and safe. Make sure you check yours out before you possibly put your health on the line.

If you do have an eating disorder, get help. Losing weight or bulking up should not be a painful and traumatizing process. The lifestyle these eating disorders necessitate are also extremely damaging to your social life. If you think you're doing this to get women or get respect, the change in your character and behavior due to what are neurotic behaviors will offset any change in your physique. If you're ever in this situation, you can get private and confidential help from the school clinic or a primary care physician to get you back on the right path.

Exercise and fitness

The second important part of maintaining health is keeping a regular exercise schedule. It's very easy to get out of shape in college and in relatively short order. The longer you wait to get into a routine, the harder it will be once you adapt a lazy and unhealthy lifestyle. Therefore, you should establish an exercise regimen as soon as you arrive on campus.

For those of us who were in high school sports, it can be difficult to do this if you're not part of a team activity. Some sports like swimming or weight lifting can be done solo. For others, you need a team. For those not on the school teams, intramural sports can be another outlet that allows you to play competitive sports, sometimes with travel to other schools. It combines the regimen and structure of team sports without the huge pressure that would come with playing for a top-level team. In Chapter 6 on extracurricular activities, intramural sports will be discussed in more detail.

As with any exercise schedule, it's best to incorporate both aerobic exercises and anaerobic exercises like strength training. One of the first things you should do coming on campus is find and understand all the options in the various campus athletic centers. Typically these are located strategically around campus to accommodate various residential areas. Usually there's a new and frequently packed athletic center and an older lesser used athletic center. The new center has the best gear, the nicest pool, and also the most people. If you are looking to meet people or play pickup basketball for example, this can be a great choice. On the other hand, during peak hours the newer gym is typically crowded to the point where you may have to wait to use a certain weight lifting machine or basketball court. Often, the older gym is not as crowded and can be a good choice if you value solitary workouts. The down side is the older gym usually has more restricted hours that may not fit your busy schedule.

In setting up an exercise schedule, the best thing to do is have days and times when you'll work out. Some people are best fresh and early in the morning while others want to wait until the evening after everything is done. Only you know what's best for you and your class and activity schedule. Often given your activities, you may have to be flexible, especially in the evenings. A good schedule is to work out at least three times a week. Setting goals for exercise and keeping track of your weight on a daily basis can help provide motivation to stick with your schedule.

Physical fitness is crucial not just because of weight concerns. Your performance on your schoolwork, your general mental well-being, sexual health, and general confidence in your physical appearance all rely on staying fit. Make fitness a part of your routine, and like good study habits, it will save you from extreme workout regimens or diets later.

Sleep

In college there's a common joke: study, party, sleep—choose two. Often the choice among students is study and party so that sleep gets the short end of the stick. Sleep is viewed as a necessary evil to prevent you from being too drowsy to function the next day. Given this perspective, it's tempting to push the boundaries of sleep as much as possible in order to maximize your time in studying and socializing.

So the question is, how much sleep do you really need? The Center for Disease Control and Prevention says adults need seven to nine hours per night. The average college student gets only six to 6.9 hours of sleep, according to a sleep fact page from the University of Michigan Health System. So it's not shocking that drowsiness, the consumption of large amounts of coffee and energy drinks, and other problems arise. The other issue is that lost sleep is a bit cumulative so that the more days you skip out on sleep, the harder you'll fall when you finally pass out.

You can't get out of sleep requirements by diet, exercise, or any sort of energy supplement. You can only delay the inevitable. Lost sleep obviously affects class performance since it can drastically reduce your attention span, but it can also affect your immunity and thus susceptibility to illness, contribute to falling into depression, and even cause automobile accidents. Therefore you should take your sleep schedule as seriously as diet or exercise in maintaining your overall health.

Granted, given the college schedule there will be exceptions. There will be five-hour nights, which can be okay as long as they're not the norm. You'll also likely pull one all-nighter, which while not healthy, is usually not a huge problem though you will be almost non-functional in your classes the next day. It's important to get sleep as soon as you can after such episodes, though it risks screwing up your sleep schedule for that night.

If you need to nap during the day, it's better to take a twenty-to-thirty minute cat nap instead of a long nap of an hour or more. Cat naps will usually help reduce most of the fatigue and not be so long that they disrupt your sleep patterns and make it difficult to get sleep that night. The best place to nap is your own room, but if you can find a safe, comfortable, and quiet place on campus for short naps this can be ideal, especially if your dorm or apartment is far from the main campus.

It's essential to get a long and good night's sleep the night before an important exam or a long-distance driving trip. Drowsiness in these situations seriously impairs your performance and can thus affect your overall grade or threaten your safety in the case of driving. In these situations, supplements such as energy drinks are no substitute for sleep since though you may stay awake and aware, your brain functions will still be impaired due to lack of sleep. In general, energy drinks are best used in moderation and in situations where detailed functioning does not matter. A good example is staying up for a party. Also, the effect of mixing energy drinks and alcohol is not fully understood but are suspected to be dangerous. Avoid these mixtures.

Illness

The first step in handling illness is prevention. The preceding sections have discussed how to have a healthy lifestyle, which boosts your immunity and makes it much less likely you'll come down with an illness. There are also other things to pay attention to in order to keep from getting sick, including washing hands before meals and not sharing cups with others.

However, the best-laid plans can sometimes fail and you may get sick. The cold or flu doesn't ask you when it comes calling, so the first thing is to be prepared. In your room it's a good idea to have a store of food, drink, and medicine for use only when you get sick. This can include soft drinks like Sprite for nausea, cans of soup and a can opener, saltine crackers, and over-the-counter painkillers, decongestants, antacids, anti-diarrheal, and symptom relievers.

In the case of medicines, be sure you get a doctor's advice on what to use instead of guessing. If you have a viral illness, antibiotics are worthless and you shouldn't take them. Also in the case of antibiotics you should take them the full time the doctor recommends, including several days after the disappearance of major symptoms in order to prevent a relapse, perhaps by a strain resistant to the antibiotic you're using. It's also important not to overuse painkillers, which can cause other health problems or even dependence in the case of prescription painkillers.

When you get sick, the most important thing is to get rest. Pushing yourself despite illness typically makes it worse and may put you out of commission for an even longer time. Also, if you're contagious, it does your fellow students no good to be coughing and sneezing in a crowded classroom. Once you fall ill, it's best to try to get rest as soon as possible to aid in your recovery. You should absolutely not drug yourself up and take stimulants or energy drinks to force yourself through the school day. This is unhealthy and even dangerous and allows the illness to get worse while only addressing superficial symptoms.

Once you're sick, it's best to stop by the school health clinic for a checkup and diagnosis. This can also get you needed prescriptions. If you have insurance or a primary care physician you're willing to pay, this is also a good option and likely much less crowded than the health clinic. If you must miss class, it's best to email the professor and/or TA as soon as possible. Give a reason for your absence, state you'll make up any assignments or tests when you can, and promise to deliver a doctor's note upon your return. You can get these from the school health clinic at the time of your visit.

At times, campuses are swept by periodic epidemics. Schools are like giant petri dishes. This can range from the flu during flu season to more insidious bugs such as mononucleosis (a.k.a. 'mono') or bacterial meningitis. There can also be STD epidemics though these are usually not public knowledge for obvious reasons. Sometimes health alerts will go out by email to the campus. If there's a mailing list from the health clinic, be sure to subscribe to get timely updates.

Other times you figure out about an outbreak from friends getting sick and decreased attendance in your classes. To limit the possibility of getting sick you can only do two things: reduce contact or decrease your susceptibility. During these times you should take extra care of your health, including eating right, taking vitamins, and washing your hands regularly. If your friends are sick it's good to help them out by bringing food, drinks, or medicine, but understand that extended contact puts you at risk. A flu vaccine may or may not protect you since the epidemic can be of a different strain than the vaccine virus. As stated before, make sure your vaccinations are up to date before going to college and check with your primary care physician to see if any other vaccinations are recommended.

Alcohol

College and alcohol are almost synonymous. Alcohol accounts for a large number of emergency room visits on college campuses, and unfortunately, also many of the deaths. Indirect effects of alcohol such as driving under the influence (DUI), fights, and unprotected sex are also hazardous to one's health. Alcohol is a drug, and it's important to know its legal uses and effects, especially if you haven't been exposed to it growing up.

First and foremost, in almost all states the drinking age is twenty-one for purchasing and consumption. So if you are under twenty-one years old, you're breaking the law and can be subject to arrest or other penalties. Granted, some of us grew up drinking at home with our families but the whole scene changes in college and even that innocuous glass of wine with dinner can get you in trouble. In addition, colleges have other penalties such as expulsion from the dorms or mandatory counseling that can kick in if you're caught drinking or even possessing alcohol. Faculty and RAs in dorms will look out for signs of intoxication and can discipline you or turn you into campus police.

There's the ideal and reality, however, so despite everyone knowing the law, there will be people who drink. In that case, the most important thing to do is practice safe behaviors. You must understand your own tolerance. This is based on the amount of alcohol you consume which depends on the type of drink and the volume you drink. A "standard drink" as a twelve-ounce beer, a five-ounce glass of wine, or 1.25 ounces of liquor like rum in a mixed drink all deliver the same amount of alcohol. So downing a few cups of heavy alcohol mixed drinks is as much alcohol as a six-pack of beer. Large mixed drinks like Long Island Iced Teas can be worth about four standard drinks *each*. Regular shots, Jell-O shots, and other types of drinks can easily have at least one standard drink or more per serving.

The standard measure of alcohol in your body is the blood alcohol concentration or BAC, which is defined as the percent of alcohol in the bloodstream by volume. Two standard drinks in one hour will raise your BAC to 0.05, so 0.05% of your blood volume will be alcohol. The standard legal limit in most states for driving is 0.08% though any BAC if you're underage can be grounds for arrest. Whether you're driving or not, however, a higher BAC increasingly impairs body functions and can lead to unconsciousness and even death from blood poisoning or choking.

Below is a list of the physiological effects of a given number of drinks over 2 hours for a 160 lb male and their various BAC levels.

2 drinks; BAC 0.02–0.03, slight euphoria

3 drinks; BAC 0.04–0.06, reduction of inhibitions, minor reasoning impairment

4 drinks; BAC 0.07–0.09, impairment of balance, speech, judgment; 0.08 is the legal limit for driving in many states.

5.5 drinks; BAC .10–.12, significant impairment of balance, etc.

7 drinks; BAC .13–.15, serious impairment of balance, etc.

8 drinks; BAC .16–.19, nausea, "sloppy" drunk

10 drinks; BAC .20–.24, disorientation, vomiting, passing out possible

12 drinks; BAC .25–.34, danger zone— severe impairment of all coordination and reasoning functions; passing out; death possible

14 drinks; BAC .35+, coma and/or death is likely

When you drink it's important to know your tolerance since everyone metabolizes alcohol a bit differently. First, weight matters, so larger people can absorb more alcohol before their BAC rises to a level a smaller person will need less drinks for. In addition, food in your stomach can help delay the absorption of alcohol, and it's best never to drink on an empty stomach. Also, don't switch between drink types frequently since this will help you get sicker and drunker. It's best to start with the more concentrated drinks first (i.e. wine, liquor), eat something in between, then go to something lighter, like beer. It's a bad idea to start at the bottom of the scale with beer and go to harder drinks since this can bring on nausea.

Often you have to be careful of delayed effects, especially if you have a lot of food in your stomach. By piling on drinks and not feeling 'drunk' you can be hit by a sudden rush of alcohol into the bloodstream due to a delayed absorption causing sudden sickness. Be careful and drink moderately, even if you don't yet feel buzzed.

If you ever find yourself drunk, it's important to remember steps to prevent injury or even death. First, stop drinking. You need to give the alcohol time to metabolize and clear your system. Only time can do this. Second, sitting down can help since you may have a loss of motor control due to the alcohol. If you have to lie down, don't do so unattended, and lie on your side, not your back, so if you vomit the vomit won't choke you. Third, only leave with people you know so you won't be taken advantage of in your condition. In addition, the friends you have watching after you should be sober.

If you have to care for a friend, stay with them and watch over them until they are sober and awake. Also, if they have irregular breathing, choke, or lose consciousness immediately call 911.

Finally, I must emphasize that it's never okay and extremely dangerous to drive under the influence. Even if you only feel 'buzzed' you may not be fit to drive and could be subject to huge penalties, including jail time and a revoked license, or worse get yourself killed or kill someone else. If you're ever unsure, wait to sober up, even if it means taking a nap in the back seat. If you need to get home or are in an unsafe area, lock your car (remember to hide all valuables) and get a ride or call a taxi. If you're sober, make sure you enforce being the designated driver and not allow others to drive you— or themselves—home drunk.

The poor feeling the morning after, commonly known as a hangover, can be the result of heavy or even light drinking. There are a lot of folk 'remedies,' but the only sound way to prevent a hangover is to either drink less or drink water progressively throughout the time when you drink to keep your body hydrated.

A final note is the dangers of alcohol and sex. Alcohol lowers inhibitions and can make us do things we would not do otherwise. Regarding sex, alcohol typically has the effect of making you less discriminating toward the opposite sex (in terms of looks, etc.) and also more likely to indulge in risky behavior such as sex with a complete stranger or unprotected sex. Even worse, alcohol can make some people more aggressive and can cause you to be accused of rape if you force someone into sex without their full, sober consent. Unless you're in a relationship, it's often best not to mix sex and drinking. Even if you're not drunk, the other party's lack of sobriety and discretion could lead to uncomfortable situations or even trouble later.

Alcohol is acceptable but must be handled in a responsible and legal fashion. Ignoring its effects and being naïve about your own 'tolerance' can have fatal effects. Have fun, but always keep this in mind.

Mental health

With all the emphasis on physical health, we can't forget the equally important mental component. Your mental health needs tending as well since it's often mental health that can make or break your time in college including academic performance, relationships, and general happiness.

One of the biggest causes of the degradation of mental health in college is stress, which can come from a confluence of factors in school, including academic, personal, relationship, and family. Stress can be defined as a pervasive situation of uncertainty, anxiety, or depression about issues impacting your life and well-being. While stress is primarily mental, it can eventually cause physical damage such as sickness. In the extreme, it can cause chronic depression, which can lead to a breakdown in many parts of your life.

Many times our lives are defined by stress, so claiming that you can escape it is deceptive. Granted, you can reduce the amount of stress you encounter. EdCon 1, where you are academically on edge, is extremely stressful but can be prevented by proper study habits. If you're in a relationship, there can be stress due to relationship problems, unexpected events like a pregnancy or a breakup. In addition, the normal aspects of social lives, finances, and family can all cause an increase in stress. This may sound like a broken record, but your stress can also increase due to poor diet, less exercise, and bad sleeping habits. These all affect your mental state.

You can't avoid stress, but the good thing is that you can manage it. The first thing you need to do is to keep your academic study habits and financial situation in as good a condition as possible. This was covered earlier, but even if you're in a situation where you take an academic or financial hit, if you have prepared, you can handle it better and reduce the subsequent stress. Second, you need to know how to relax. If you are working constantly, there's a limit to how much information your brain will take in. You need to get up and take a break, walking around, playing video games, or even hanging with friends.

Once the Dalai Lama visited Taiwan and was asked what he would tell someone considering suicide. His response was to take a nap. One of the best ways to get rid of stress in an immediate fashion is to go to sleep. For some reason, sleep can often reduce a sense of hopelessness and being overwhelmed. A close second can be exercise, which often can work to clear the mind or even help you solve what seems like an intractable problem. Other relaxing activities include pleasure reading, which often works to clear the mind before studying, leisurely walks, meditation, or even movies.

Finally, talking to people you trust can also help put your stress in perspective. These could be friends, parents, RAs, or even professors. Dozens of college students commit suicide every year. One wonders whether they actually talked to someone who could emphasize that college, even bad grades in college, is not the end of the world and is even small in the larger scheme of things. The girlfriend you could be obsessed over may only be a bump on the road to meeting someone even better. You're not the only one who has gone through these sorts of situations, and many people have survived much worse (think slavery or segregation). Putting things in perspective can help immensely in reducing stress and placing priorities correctly.

Schools also have professional resources to help students handle stress. These can include hotlines or counselors. If you really feel you need help, there should be no stigma to seeing a counselor. It does not make you a 'nut' or a loser. There is a particular stigma in the Black community toward mental health professionals and plenty of people do not get help when they could use it. You can often visit anonymously and they are legally required to keep your comments confidential.

The most important thing though is to not give up! You can get through this, and you can succeed despite whatever odds seem stacked against you. It may mean that you need help—we all need help at times. It also may mean you can't be perfect in everything. What you can do though is to find out how to manage your life and achieve your goals by prioritizing them and placing them in the right perspective.

Depression

Depression typically doesn't just mean a bad day. It often means a chronic condition where a near continuous state of depression defines your mental state. The danger of depression is that it often leads to a greater sense of helplessness where you gradually let your life fall apart, fall away from friends, lovers, and school, and in the most extreme case, consider suicide.

Depression is often unrecognized in Black men and comes with a stigma. John Head, author of *Standing in the Shadows: Understanding and Overcoming Depression in Black Men*, talks about his experience with depression in his book, including nearly committing suicide. Often depression signs are unrecognized or ignored and can get worse over time. Depression can also affect any part of our community from those under the poverty line to the more affluent, so social class is not necessarily the best indicator of a risk factor.

If you're depressed almost continuously and seeking advice and counsel from family and friends is inadequate, you may have clinical depression and need to seek out a mental health professional. Again, there's nothing wrong with doing this. If you don't feel comfortable with seeing a professional on campus, you can look up a professional in the local community who is unaffiliated with the school.

Suicide—don't do it

A teacher I once had said it best about suicide: "Suicide is a permanent solution to a temporary problem." Indeed it is, and it's becoming increasingly prevalent in the Black community. Another, less reverent view of suicide was once taken by Chris Rock who once joked about the difference in suicide rates between Blacks and Whites. The gist of the joke was Black kids in the projects with damaged families and lives don't take their own lives as fast as suburban White kids who can't get a new car. The fact that there are different suicide rates between Blacks and Whites is true, though this gap is narrowing. Despite this, the college years show one of the highest jumps in the suicide rate of any age. The graph below shows the most recent (2007) suicide rates (per 100,000 people) by Black males between ages 15-19 as well as 20-24.

There is a doubling of suicide as a risk factor for the cause of death as you go into your college years. Somehow, taking one's own life becomes an attractive option for more people around age 20.

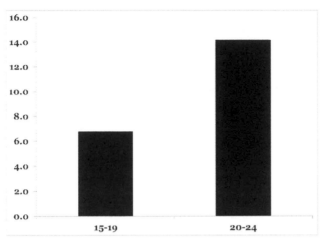

FIGURE 5: Suicide rate for Black American males ages 15-19 and 20-24 per 100,000 persons. Source: CDC

Despite the jokes, Blacks do commit suicide over as trivial reasons as Whites. Remember, suicide is never an option. If you're ever considering it, you should see a mental health professional immediately. If one isn't accessible, there are many hotlines, like the National Suicide Prevention hotline at 1-800-273-8255, you can call that are anonymous and can help you think through the immediate issue bringing on your bout with suicide. You don't have to deal with it alone, and it's best you don't. At the end of the day, if the choice is between taking a break from school and taking your own life, take the former. At least you can always go back to school.

Sex and sexually transmitted diseases

So you met one of the finest dimes ever at this party. Beautiful, smart, funny and she seems to have a good heart as well. Better yet, she is "down."

So you go back and do your thing. No condom was available, but hey you didn't like them anyway. This isn't one of the ditzy girls or slutty types, so why worry? A few weeks down the line you notice problems in certain places and realize you made a bit of a mistake. Maybe she knew, maybe she didn't. What matters is you now have an appointment with the doctor and you better hope you have something of the treatable variety. What's worse is you see her the next day and she informs you she has missed her period. Man, aren't you lucky?

Sex is a natural part of life. However, a lot of people seem to lose any sense of maturity and responsibility when dealing with it. Face it, when you fantasize about sex it is about the act, the good stuff. It isn't about the awkward morning after, the sexually transmitted disease (STD), the accidental pregnancy, or the vengeful boyfriend you never knew she had. Because of the idealization, sometimes you can trip up on the reality.

STDs and pregnancy are two of the largest downsides from irresponsible sex. You would think with the modern emphasis on sex education and the sex all over the media that people would understand and be more careful in their sexual relations. Unfortunately, they are still as reckless as ever. Despite what people think to the contrary, I haven't seen any lack of recklessness around sex despite age, race, education, or income. I think overall maturity and sometimes religious conviction are the biggest moderating factors I've seen, though even these are inconsistent.

I won't give an academic discussion of all the different STDs since you can find that pretty easily via Google. They are caused by all kinds of organisms from bacteria to viruses to insects (pubic lice a.k.a. crabs). Most are bacteria, such as gonorrhea and syphilis and are treatable using antibiotics. However, like many diseases, antibiotic resistance is appearing, and it's no longer as easy as getting a shot of penicillin to get off the hook. Others are a bit more difficult. The herpes virus, while not fatal, cannot be cured and will recur throughout your life. HIV, while not the automatic death sentence it once was, will condemn you to a lifetime of expensive drug therapy and probably a bad sex life since you would have to tell all potential partners your HIV-positive status.

Sadly STDs are very prominent in the Black community, usually at multiple the rates for Whites and other ethnic groups. For the two most common, Chlamydia and gonorrhea, the rates near 1,000 cases per 100,000 people or one out of 100 according to the CDC. Given there are few outward signs and symptoms, you really don't know who these people are. Don't try to guess. Keep safe.

About preventing STDs, there's not much to say. Always use protection. Always. You should know how to use a condom and also the strengths and weaknesses of each type. For example, the lambskin condoms prevent pregnancy but not STDs. The typical reasons for not using one don't add up to the risks. Here are a few:

> 1. "I don't like condoms." That's nice. I hope you like bratty kids and crabs since these are the alternatives you're rolling dice with every time you smash. Just remember, even if your partner has only slept with one other person, you are essentially screwing the chain of partners that stretches between

everyone her previous partner slept with. These days, this reckless behavior is less of an excuse since there are so many types of condoms of different materials (latex, ultra-thin polymers, animal skin) with different sizes and thicknesses. Even if you have to go mail order, you can find one that works.

2. "She doesn't like condoms." Well, you're the man, aren't you, and it takes two to screw. Also, do you think you are the first dude she has told this to?

3. "She says she is on birth control." Two things factor in. First, what if she messes up? Misses some doses or takes the placebo at the wrong time. Then she can get pregnant. In that case it isn't all her fault because you had to help! Second, is she really on the pill or something else? Girls lie, especially if they think that getting pregnant can keep you together. In the worst case if you're successful, be it in sports or a career, this one mistake can trap people in a relationship or a life of child support. Yes, people are that devious.

4. "All my friends don't do it." Your friends are idiots (at least as far as safe sex is concerned). Ignore them on this point or get new ones. Sorry, that's how it is.

5. "I have latex allergies." There are other polymers in use now. You don't have to use latex.

6. "It's embarrassing to buy condoms at the drug store, especially if they have to open the glass cabinet." Condoms are some of the most often shoplifted items and are sometimes under lock and key. If this is a real issue for you, buy them online. Again though, what's worse, being embarrassed or getting a girl knocked up?

I take a hard line on this because I have seen too many people get caught. Now they're dealing with a lifetime herpes infection or a child from a woman they now hate.

On a final note, it is good to use protection, but be careful if you don't trust the girl. If you have any suspicions, make sure you dispose of the condom yourself. In the NFL, players are advised to always dispose of condoms themselves since sports groupies have tried to use leftover semen in condoms to get pregnant. Also, always have your own condom on hand. While it's okay to accept condoms from the girl, you have no idea how it's been stored and handled. Yes, there are people devious enough to poke holes in condoms and still smile in your face. This can happen to college athletes or those with a bright future as well so keep on your toes.

Pregnancy

The next big danger from sex to your health is pregnancy. Men obviously don't get pregnant, but getting someone else pregnant can seriously screw up your life and affect your health. The steps above on condoms can be used to prevent pregnancy and you need to make sure both you and your partner are down with these. If something happens, for example a condom fails, there's no need to panic. There are over-the-counter morning-after pills now available at most pharmacies that can prevent pregnancy if taken in the first twenty-four or forty-eight hours.

However, if you do mess up and a girl gets pregnant, deal with it in a mature and responsible manner. Don't leave her in the lurch, even if you can't tolerate her. This is your fault too, so you need to man up and take responsibility. How and when to tell both of your families is up to you, but you can't keep them in the dark forever. After the initial blow-up they will possibly provide needed support.

Terminating the pregnancy is a deep decision that can only be considered by you both in terms of your religious values and the safety of such an act given the progress of the pregnancy. There's always the option of putting a child up for adoption if you bring him or her to term. You will likely want to discuss this with a variety of people, including your family, any older people you respect, health care professionals, religious figures, family planning centers, or friends you know who have been through the same situation.

One of the biggest decisions you'll need to make is how to continue your education after becoming a parent. You should take any and every step you can to finish your education since a common regret I've heard is that someone leaves school when they have a kid and live with the regret and reduced opportunities that result for the rest of their life. You can go to school and be a parent but it's easier if both parents are involved and help each other. Otherwise, your family can provide valuable help. If they are supportive enough they can even raise the kid until you get out.

If you become a father, act like a father. Do everything you can to stay in your kid's life. There are enough people growing up in our community who never knew their father and you don't need to augment the statistic. There are ways to be with your kid, even if you aren't married to the mother, but you must have the will to do so and the courage to devote most of your life to give the child a fighting chance.

Illegal drugs

Illegal drugs are a step up from alcohol. One could argue that the drug war is ineffective, treats the criminal and not public health aspects of drug use, and has an absolutely malicious effect on the American population, particularly the Black community. But this is not the place for such debates nor are we going to downplay the effects of drugs such as marijuana just because they are popular. The fact is illegal drug use can damage your college career in many ways, and it's advisable to stay away from controlled substances. If you want to be more libertarian minded, fine, just don't be shocked at what can happen when you get caught.

Illegal drug use spans dozens of different types of substances, and in general, these can be absolutely illegal substances like marijuana and cocaine, legal drugs that are misused such as prescription drugs like the prescription stimulant Adderall, and abuse of completely unrelated substances that nevertheless give you a high. I hope no one sniffs glue in college but you never know.

Drugs are abused because they produce a certain effect for a person that is difficult or impossible for them to obtain otherwise. Usually these are a high feeling (followed by a down) or sometimes 'performance enhancement' such as using Adderall to stimulate yourself into studying all night. I'm not going to go into the whole pitch on 'Just Say No'. Also, the effects of drugs are something you can easily look up. If you're college age and have gone through any kind of schooling, this has probably been repeated ad nauseam.

If you don't have a strong will or are vulnerable to peer pressure, college can get you into trouble. There are more and different types of drugs since dealers gravitate toward college areas. Often the dealers are students themselves. There is a wider social clique where drugs may be seen as an acceptable 'lifestyle choice' and you can just hang in those circles to puff or snort without the guilt. Unlike high school, no one is going to hold your hand or even always tell your parents. You are an adult now and the temptation is yours to take or refuse.

This may be seen as an upside for those who want more freedom, but it also means no one is going to stop your life from going into a downward spiral until you hit the bottom. You don't have to go there, and it's ridiculous to think your social life needs anything like these substances. I got through college (and life) without touching them, and so can you. If you're taking drugs to make you forget your problems, drugs always make them worse. If you have financial problems, well, do you think dime bags are free? Also, remember if you're dealing, you could lose all of your federal financial aid. Don't even think drugs are going to help you succeed more in school. If you need stimulants to cram for a test, you're trying to cover up a semester of mistakes with a magic cure. It won't work in the long run.

Then there is the whole criminal record and jail thing. Never mind you can be kicked out of school, you could end up with a record and all the things that go with it. Congrats, you are now a statistic. Great luck putting this background on a job application. Even if you aren't caught, many employers routinely ask for drug tests so you have to hope and pray that it's out of your system. Feel like losing your dream internship or job for a few hours on the bong?

Everyone makes mistakes though, and if you ever think you have a drug problem, it's important to get help. There are many professional help resources both on campus and through organizations like Addicts Anonymous who can help you with both the psychological and physical aspects of breaking the addiction. Again, if you need help there should be no stigma.

On the flip side of drug addiction is drug dealing. This has been seen by many a college student as a way to make ends meet, or more often, a way to live a lavish lifestyle they could otherwise not support. I've never met a drug dealer who bragged about funneling all his proceeds to the school bursar. Drug dealing at school is hazardous for several reasons. First, you're in an environment that likely has a large law enforcement and student enforcement (think RAs) presence. You can easily be caught, especially if you try to get big. Second, being in college doesn't make you immune to the robberies, fights, or shootings that encumber drug dealers elsewhere. Some people brag they have private connections, for example, to funnel drugs to frat parties. Again, if the frat is busted, do you think they would blink an eye before naming you to the cops? Dealing drugs, unlike using them, is also a one-way ticket home with no refund.

If you need the money, there are plenty of legitimate ways to get it at school as was discussed in Chapter 3 on finances. Again, why are you in college paying tens of thousands of dollars per year to sling dope, which will probably only net you a few thousand dollars?

Chronic health issues

In this last part of the health section we address those who have long-term health issues they'll have to deal with in school. Some of these are pretty normal like asthma or allergies while others can be very difficult such as genetic disorders like sickle cell anemia. You have the right to enjoy college and live a normal life like everyone else, but keeping all other health issues in mind, you must make sure your care and treatment do not suffer due to the college lifestyle.

First, if you have to make regular doctor visits, make sure you get a referral to a good clinician in the area who can serve you. Often university hospitals have the right kinds of people but you don't have to limit yourself to them. Don't skip out on or reduce the number of appointments you go to. If you have cancer or a heart condition and need to go for a monitoring visit every few months, schedule it early so it doesn't conflict with exams, trips, or anything else. When you arrive on campus you should file your illness with the school clinic so they'll know how to help you if you need it and make you aware of campus support systems.

Second, make sure you have your 'emergency' needs on hand and have someone who can help you in an emergency. For asthmatics this can mean having an inhaler with you at all times or even a nebulizer in your room. For sickle cell, you know you may have acute pain episodes so make sure you have the right medications or can arrange to get to a hospital that can best treat your symptoms if they occur.

Finally, do not do anything, even in the name of fun, that can worsen your condition. Take your medicines on time and on schedule, maintain a proper diet that avoids things you can't eat and includes things you must eat, deal with the symptoms as soon as they appear, and keep yourself out of tempting situations that can get you in trouble. One aspect of college that may help is that there could be a support group of people who suffer from the same malady. This can help bring you together and create a support system of friends on campus.

Safety

If you can keep yourself healthy, it will still be all for naught if you can't stay safe. Safety is probably something your parent(s) or guardians were paranoid about before you went to school. It can be a huge issue on college campuses. The horror stories of injuries and deaths that you hear about regarding college students are a very small probability for the average student but are still a real possibility. One of the problems though is that compared to health, safety can have many more aspects, not all of which are obvious. There's the basic campus safety and street smarts but also safety at parties, online, on dates, dealing with law enforcement, and even firearms can all come into play.

Basic safety

Basic safety in the minds of most people is keeping out of the wrong place at the wrong time. Today's campuses are huge, well-lit, and well policed but that doesn't mean they are impregnable. On many campuses, right outside the campus boundaries are unsafe areas. Many students unintentionally forget they aren't living in the boondocks and go jogging at 11:00 P.M. with their iPod on the borders of campus or off campus and are shocked when they get robbed. There's no bigger way to say "I'm an easy target."

Knowing your campus and its environs are essential and are something you can find out in your first weeks. Often you can ask upperclassmen as well as campus police where most of the incidents happen and what to watch out for. Another good source people don't know about is taxi drivers. Talking to a taxi driver can give you some of the best and up-to-date information about the surrounding area.

Regardless, it's usually not a good idea to wander alone at night unless you're on a main section of campus that is well lit, monitored, and populated by people. It's a bit easier as a guy but guys can still get targeted. Walking around off campus at night is usually not a good idea. Maybe you are street smart and came from a rough neighborhood, but usually mitigating risk instead of inviting an incident is the best policy. If in doubt, always get a ride.

You have to learn to be street smart and aware. Always be knowledgeable of your surroundings. It reduces your awareness and thieves know this. In addition, off campus you sometimes need to watch wearing university gear. This is usually harmless, but if someone wants to target a student—someone who usually isn't as knowledgeable of the area and likely has money—you instantly identify yourself. This is especially true when jogging around off-campus. The same rules about talking to strangers can apply as well. College campuses seem to attract a lot of weirdos for some reason so you may want to be careful who you talk to and how much personal information you divulge. You are under no obligation to tell anyone anything.

Party safety

Nothing can be safer than going to a party with your friends and hanging out, right? Well, not always. First, whenever you go to a party, someone in your group who you trust should know the person throwing the party. There are exceptions such as parties sponsored by frats or campus groups and in your first year you may not know as many people. You need to know what you're getting into though. If you walk in and people are popping ecstasy and snorting coke, you could be in a potentially volatile situation. Anything could happen— from fights to shootings to a police raid.

Next, when you are at a party, even one thrown by someone you know, you have to be extremely cautious about drinking anything you did not see opened or mixed with your own eyes, especially if someone you don't know gives it to you. There are a lot of cases, not always publicized, of punch bowl drinks being spiked as a prank, as a way to get the party 'moving', or out of malice. These drinks can also have an obscenely high alcohol content that is disguised by lots of flavoring and sugar. The safest thing to always do is to drink something you've seen opened, mix your own drink from the Coke, rum, vodka or whatever, or bring your own stuff. It may seem 'lame' to do so, but knowing what you are drinking should always be in the back of your mind. Granted if you're at a party where everyone is good friends, it's different from a party where you only know two people, but never be naïve, even in this situation. Following on this, it is pretty unsanitary to share cups with people. Get your own cup.

Intoxication was covered in health but again make sure you stay in control when drinking. Passing out at a party is dangerous and not a good way to make an impression. You can wake up the next morning missing money, credit cards, jewelry, and even sexually molested. Drink (if you are above 21) and have fun, but be responsible.

Drinking typically leads to another safety issue: fights. It takes nothing but a bit of alcohol to make some people incredibly belligerent and willing to fight over words, spilling your drink on them, a girl, or anything else trivial.

If someone is intoxicated and looks ready to fight, it's best to swallow your pride and remove yourself from the situation. They aren't thinking straight and are unpredictable. If you see a fight break out, it's usually not a good idea to stand around watching and cheering. Besides the moral aspect, there are a lot of guys who'll try to win a fight by pulling out a gun and often bystanders get shot. In addition, if the guy has a crew he hangs with, they could get into the fight, making it a mass brawl. Then the police arrive and it can get ugly.

Online safety

Online safety is a bigger concern now than when I went to school. Yeah, there were weirdos and perverts on AOL Instant Messenger and Usenet bulletin boards but they typically knew nothing but what you were dumb enough to divulge. Now with Facebook, LinkedIn, and other social networking sites, they can learn a frightening amount of information about you without even contacting you.

Online safety will be covered in detail in Chapter 10 on technology, but the theme is similar to that of overall safety. Make sure you can control who has access to your personal information, both by what you put out there and how you protect it. Remember, much of the information posted on the Internet never leaves!

Law enforcement

Law enforcement is around to uphold the laws and public safety, and the vast majority of them perform this task admirably. However, as a Black male you should know that you can be open to profiling, targeting, or even harassment by some members of law enforcement. These situations can happen anywhere from traffic stops to raids on parties to police coming to your dorm room.

In all of these cases, the wrong moves by you can lead to escalated penalties by the police officer or even injury. Here, we'll discuss your rights and also what's appropriate behavior. The most important things that many people still don't understand is to keep your mouth shut, follow directions, and do not make any threatening moves. You don't want to end up like many other innocent shooting victims. The best guide for this I have found is the American Civil Liberties Union (ACLU)'s Bust Card, which describes your rights and proper actions when pulled over by police. It's available online at http://www.aclu.org/issues/criminal/bustcardtext .html, but we also reprint it with permission below:

WHAT TO DO IF YOU'RE STOPPED BY POLICE, IMMIGRATION AGENTS OR THE FBI

YOUR RIGHTS

> You have the right to remain silent. If you wish to exercise that right, say so out loud.

> You have the right to refuse to consent to a search of yourself, your car, or your home.

> If you are not under arrest, you have the right to calmly leave.

> You have the right to a lawyer if you are arrested. Ask for one immediately.

> Regardless of your immigration or citizenship status, you have constitutional rights.

YOUR RESPONSIBILITIES

> Do stay calm and be polite.

Do not interfere with or obstruct the police.

Do not lie or give false documents.

Do prepare yourself and your family in case you are arrested.

Do remember the details of the encounter.

Do file a written complaint or call your local ACLU if you feel your rights have been violated.

IF YOU ARE STOPPED FOR QUESTIONING

Stay calm. Don't run. Don't argue, resist, or obstruct the police, even if you are innocent or police are violating your rights. Keep your hands where the police can see them.

Ask if you are free to leave. If the officer says yes, calmly and silently walk away. If you are under arrest, you have a right to know why.

You have the right to remain silent and cannot be punished for refusing to answer questions. If you wish to remain silent, tell the officer out loud. In some states, you must give your name if asked to identify yourself.

You do not have to consent to a search of yourself or your belongings, but police may "pat down" your clothing if they suspect a weapon. You should not physically resist, but you have the right to refuse consent for any further search. If you do consent, it can affect you later in court.

IF YOU ARE STOPPED IN YOUR CAR

Stop the car in a safe place as quickly as possible. Turn off the car, turn on the internal light, open the window part way, and place your hands on the wheel.

Upon request, show police your driver's license, registration and proof of insurance.

If an officer or immigration agent asks to look inside your car, you can refuse to consent to the search, but if police believe your car contains evidence of a crime, your car can be searched without your consent.

Both drivers and passengers have the right to remain silent. If you are a passenger, you can ask if you are free to leave. If the officer says yes, sit silently or calmly leave. Even if the officer says no, you have the right to remain silent.

IF YOU ARE QUESTIONED ABOUT YOUR IMMIGRATION STATUS

You have the right to remain silent and do not have to discuss your immigration or citizenship status with police, immigration agents, or any other officials. You do not have to answer questions about where you were born, whether you are a U.S. citizen, or how you entered the country. (Separate rules apply at international borders and airports, and for individuals on certain nonimmigrant visas, including tourists and business travelers.)

If you are not a U.S. citizen and an immigration agent requests your immigration papers, you must show them if you have them with you. If you are over 18, carry your immigration documents with you at all times. If you do not have immigration papers, say you want to remain silent.

Do not lie about your citizenship status or provide fake documents.

IF THE POLICE OR IMMIGRATION AGENTS COME TO YOUR HOME

If the police or immigration agents come to your home, you do not have to let them in unless they have certain kinds of warrants.

Ask the officer to slip the warrant under the door or hold it up to the window so you can inspect it. A search warrant allows police to enter the address listed on the warrant, but officers can only search the areas and for the items listed. An arrest warrant allows police to enter the home of the person listed on the warrant if they believe the person is inside. A warrant of removal/deportation (Immigration and Customs Enforcement (ICE) warrant) does not allow officers to enter a home without consent.

Even if officers have a warrant, you have the right to remain silent. If you choose to speak to the officers, step outside and close the door.

IF YOU ARE CONTACTED BY THE FBI

If an FBI agent comes to your home or workplace, you do not have to answer any questions. Tell the agent you want to speak to a lawyer first.

If you are asked to meet with FBI agents for an interview, you have the right to say you do not want to be interviewed. If you agree to an interview, have a lawyer present. You do not have to answer any questions you feel uncomfortable answering, and can say that you will only answer questions on a specific topic.

IF YOU ARE ARRESTED

Do not resist arrest, even if you believe the arrest is unfair.

Say you wish to remain silent and ask for a lawyer immediately. Don't give any explanations or excuses. If you can't pay for a lawyer, you have the right to a free one. Don't say anything, sign anything or make any decisions without a lawyer.

You have the right to make a local phone call. The police cannot listen if you call a lawyer.

Prepare yourself and your family in case you are arrested. Memorize the phone numbers of your family and your lawyer. Make emergency plans if you have children or take medication.

Special considerations for non-citizens:

> Ask your lawyer about the effect of a criminal conviction or plea on your immigration status.

> Don't discuss your immigration status with anyone but your lawyer.

> While you are in jail, an immigration agent may visit you. Do not answer questions or sign anything before talking to a lawyer.

> Read all papers fully. If you do not understand or cannot read the papers, tell the officer you need an interpreter.

IF YOU FEEL YOUR RIGHTS HAVE BEEN VIOLATED

> Remember: police misconduct cannot be challenged on the street. Don't physically resist officers or threaten to file a complaint.

> Write down everything you remember, including officers' badge and patrol car numbers, which agency the officers were from, and any other details. Get contact information for witnesses. If you are injured, take photographs of your injuries (but seek medical attention first).

> File a written complaint with the agency's internal affairs division or civilian com-

plaint board. In most cases, you can file a complaint anonymously if you wish.

Call your local ACLU or visit www.aclu.org/profiling.

All of this is not official legal advice, but it is a good guide on how to act. Don't mouth off or otherwise cause trouble. Sometimes it's better to back down and live to fight another day. If you see others arrested or having issues, do not intervene. The time of arrest or questioning can be very volatile, so it's best to toe a straight line and look for options to redress the grievance later.

Firearms safety

Some of us own guns (legally) and the question may arise if you can have it on campus. It's important to be aware of school regulations in this regard. Usually campuses do not allow firearms in campus buildings, including dorms. If you have a residence off campus you will likely be able to keep a firearm in accordance with local laws. However, if you are in a different state than where you grew up, be sure to be familiar with local gun laws, including concealed carry.

If you have a concealed carry permit, usually requiring you to be at least twenty-one, some states have reciprocity for other states' permits. You should look at the laws in detail, and ask local law enforcement if you aren't sure. There are also often city laws that are stricter than state laws so you need to know those too. Make sure you know the laws on storing or transporting firearms since some states or cities may require the guns to be stored or transported locked and unloaded.

As far as gun safety, make sure you have had a basic firearms course (these can be given by local ranges and certified by the National Rifle Association) and read a book on safety for the firearms you own. You should only shoot your gun at an authorized range and not in public lands unless you have a permit for activities like hunting. You should refresh yourself on the basics of gun safety every year or so to make sure you do not have an accident. Finally, you need to be cautious in who you tell about firearms. Tell no one unless they need to know. Never, ever lend out your firearm to anyone, even someone you trust. You don't want to be caught if your gun is used in a crime or sold and is traced back to you.

Safety in large-scale disasters

We live in a turbulent world and there are many disasters—both natural and man-made that can strike without notice. They range from Xavier University students dealing with Hurricane Katrina to New York University students who were in the city on 9/11 (I was a senior, but not in NY, then). Large-scale disasters are rare and huge in scope, which means their accurate prediction over short time scales is nearly impossible. Since we can't predict, we must prepare and be ready to act if there's trouble.

Large-scale disasters can strike anywhere or anytime. Some areas are more prone to certain natural disasters than others. For example, hurricanes are more common in Miami, tornadoes more common in Oklahoma, and earthquakes are more common in the San Francisco Bay Area. There is also the possibility of man-made disasters such as terrorism, riots, or mass electrical blackouts. Man-made disasters typically, but not always, are more impactful in urban areas than rural ones. All of these though can require some of the same preparation.

In short, you need to be prepared to support yourself and maybe your roommates through a period that can be a couple of days or longer. Many schools have disaster preparedness plans, and it may behoove you to look them up to be aware of what's expected. However, to prepare for the worst you need to assume you need food, water, medicine, and communications until help arrives or you are evacuated by school, state, or federal authorities.

First, you need a first aid kit, regardless if you are expecting a disaster. These are relatively inexpensive at most drug stores. You should get the larger ones though with band aids, gauze, and basic medicine to make sure you have all the major supplies. Next, you need temporary supplies of food and water. Each person needs about a gallon of water per day—about eight bottles of water. So having one flat of about thirty bottles of water should suffice for several days. Next is food. You should have some canned food on hand anyway in case of illness but these will typically be soup. Also keeping cans (don't forget a can-opener!) of beans and vegetables, as well as some meat like tuna or sardines and granola bars on hand can give you some options in case there are some issues. Be sure to keep this food on hand for only emergencies and don't munch on it randomly. Finally, make sure you have a flashlight and a radio along with two sets of batteries for each. The radio should be AM/FM but having shortwave reception is a big plus.

In case of a disaster, it's best to wait where you are for the authorities or other instructions. In case of large disasters, there could be a communications outage since cell phone towers and phone landlines only have a limited capacity. In this case, where phone and Internet are not available, the only option you'll have is radio. CB radios are relatively cheap and don't require a license. A ham radio license, which no longer requires Morse code, is even better but may not be up your alley. One tip is to see if the university has a ham radio club and to know the location of the equipment. In an adverse situation, the club may help you use the equipment to receive news or communicate. If there is no university ham club, keep the phone and address of a local ham radio club handy and contact them if necessary. It may be a long shot but it may also be the only two-way communication option you have besides passively listening to the radio.

Conclusion

Your health and safety are your responsibility, and you must take them seriously. College can be great fun and eye opening but be sure to keep your wits about you and keep yourself in good physical and mental health to maximize your enjoyment of your time there.

Chapter 6
Extracurricular Activities

The function of the university is not simply to teach breadwinning, or to furnish teachers for the public schools, or to be a centre of polite society; it is, above all, to be the organ of that fine adjustment between real life and the growing knowledge of life, an adjustment from which forms the secret of civilization.
—W.E.B. DuBois

For many, extracurriculars dominate their college experience. Be it student government, the student paper, political groups, or fraternities they spend almost every waking moment outside of class in these activities. Some people opt out and would rather chill with friends or play World of Warcraft. Most people dabble in extracurriculars to some extent though. There's a lot out there, and there's a way to maximize what you get from these endeavors. In this chapter, we will cover the different types of extracurriculars and talk about how to maximize your participation.

Unfortunately, I won't be covering fraternities, Black or not. I didn't pledge undergrad and I don't think I would be the best source for advice or information. There have been some good books like *Black Greek 101* by Walter Kimbrough that describe the history and culture of the Divine Nine (nine traditional Black fraternities and sororities) so I would direct you there. Likewise, not having experience with majority White fraternities I can't speak to their inner practices, treatment of Black members, etc. I know many people who have been happy as brothers of non-Black fraternities and some who have disliked it, and their experience can vary by fraternity and campus. Likewise there are some proud non-Black members of the Divine Nine, which shows how the cultural capital of these fraternities is becoming more widespread and respected.

Student government

Student government probably stands at the top in terms of prestige on campus. Its actual impact may vary by campus but no one denies these are competitive positions given the large-scale voting and campaigning and the complex issues involved. Typically there's the student government, which runs student affairs at a university, a sort of adjudication or conflict resolution organization, and other bodies, such as campus honor systems to uphold certain university norms.

First off, if you want to get involved in these you must decide early and be serious. Campaigning can take a lot of time and effort, even for minimal posts. Granted, you could run unopposed but don't count on it. In short you need three things: a platform, a message, and a support network. Your platform is your plan, which must be in writing. It talks about what you see as the most important issues and your concrete plan on resolving them. Second is your message, which is how you carry your platform to possible voters. Unfortunately, people have short attention spans, so messages tend to be sound-bite length. The Internet Age is not kind to Abraham Lincoln or Martin Luther King Jr. style oratory. Finally, you need a support network. These people help campaign for you and may later help you implement or gain consensus on implementing your platform.

It can help to learn how to debate, collaborate, or stand your ground as part of the political process. Always remember who you were elected to represent and to whom you are ultimately accountable. In the end, the flash may get you elected but what you do endures more and reflects more on your reputation. Also, in elections always read the rules on campaigning, funding, etc., carefully. You would not want your budding political career to be wrecked by minor technicalities.

Student groups

There are a plethora of student groups at most modern universities, ranging from the cultural to political to ethnic to school major. I couldn't even list a fraction here. In general, they appeal to members with a shared interest in the purpose of the group and its activities on and off campus. Some groups are campus specific while many are appendages of national organizations or movements.

On the more scholarly end there are groups oriented toward students with a particular major like physics, English, or economics. These are often attended by members of the major to explore relevant topics in more depth, bring in prominent guest speakers, and assist in career aspirations. There can also be events with a more competitive bent like mock trial, debate, or academic bowl–like competitions where you compete to answer questions in a quiz-bowl type format.

Political groups tend to be focused around political parties, leaders, or a specific ideology. College campuses are full of open-minded and impressionable students so you find everything from the objectivist followers of Ayn Rand to the worker's party/socialist type organizations. These can range from private discussions on politics to participation in larger campaigns or activism. Typically, many Black students will be more active in organizations that tend to be liberal or have viewpoints they interpret as benign to Black interests. This is fine, however, whatever your political affiliation, college is one of the few times in life it will be easy to see what someone else's views are in an open environment. I went to campus speakers from the libertarians, Republicans, and the socialists. I feel I was better having the perspectives, and even if you don't agree with their stance, you can at least be more educated about what it really is instead of having someone tell you.

Likewise, if your political or ideological preference diverges from your friends' or community's, there's nothing to be ashamed of or worried about in participating in a group you're passionate about or even trying to teach your friends your point of view. Blacks have been part of pretty much every major political movement in history. If you don't believe me go to Google and type in "Black populists" or "Blacks and Greenback Party." The problem typically comes in one of the two A's: arrogance and aloofness. First, just because you have different views, arrogance should not be used as a defense mechanism to deprecate other Blacks, or other people in general who don't agree with you.

This negative trait will only reinforce hostile opinions.

Second, don't lapse into aloofness where you claim you have to separate yourself from the Black community because of your views. Stand tall and toughen up. People may disagree with you, just defend yourself if challenged. Don't cast off all Blacks as some monolithic entity trying to suppress your individualism. They have as much right to their opinion as you do yours. There are some people who complain of persecution yet attack their opponents even more viciously when given a chance. Don't be one of these. If you ever have a disagreement, there's nothing more disarming than asking someone to sit down and explain what they mean. Either they can't, and your argument is half won, or you may gain someone who respects you, even if they don't agree.

Ethnic organizations

Ethnic groups are another prominent type of organization on campus. If you're reading this book you probably are Black and the Black organizations on campus hold the most attraction. I was a member of several Black organizations and president of one, Brothers United Celebrating Knowledge and Success (B.U.C.K.S.), a service organization at UVA. These organizations can be good things for the community if they address key issues and provide a forum for what may have otherwise been ignored or overlooked. They hold a special place on campus in good and bad ways.

First, if they do well they can significantly help improve the lives of many students. If they do poorly, they can often be highlighted by others, including campus media, as an example of a bad group, or worse a detriment to campus race relations.

The group should be clear from the outset what its goal is. No group can do everything. If political activism is your thing, focus on that. If it is service and education, focus on that. Above all, focus on real issues and not what is sexy or controversial to get attention. Beating on Black Women or Men constantly may make headlines but does little to solve the collective problem. Also, make membership and attendance open to all since there's no better target for criticism than an exclusionary minority organization. You should also build links with other organizations, ethnic or not, to build coalitions and hold events on campus of mutual interest.

Black organizations must also be careful. They are always under scrutiny and can sometimes fall afoul of being called too radical, nationalist, etc. Unless you're at an HBCU, always remember the larger context of existing on a majority White campus. Whenever you make a statement, particularly about other organizations or groups, imagine what your response would be if this came from a non-Black person. If you wouldn't find it acceptable, you may want to be careful how you phrase things. Many people don't have much experience around Blacks and have a different idea of what is radical. I'm not advocating watering down your message or abandoning goals to make other people happy. I'm just advising you that in order to be effective and have influence, you must be savvy. Besmirching the name of the organization in meaningless battles doesn't help your overall cause.

Another thing Black organizations should best learn is media relations. Political groups are expert at this. Sometimes instead of protests or loud denunciations, you should write guest editorials in college papers, letters to the editor, or create informational programs for students or faculty. Helping the faculty deal with politically incorrect situations, advising and supporting student government political candidates (not necessarily Black), and distributing official press releases are all effective tactics to get the word out. Otherwise you may risk appearing in an article about angry Blacks devoid of context, information, and compassion.

It's a good idea to attend events from other organizations, be they East Asians, White ethnics, Indians, Hillel, or country-based groups. Not only does this expand your horizons but you may meet new friends with whom you have a lot in common but would not encounter otherwise. Trust me, there could be few other times in life you'll get to do the Indian dance Garba-Raas or attend a Passover Seder.

Artistic groups

If you play an instrument, love to act, or just love to discuss literature, these groups may be for you. Granted, if you're practicing and doing performances these groups can be time consuming but well worth it. One of the first things people realize in college is that the arts are on another level than high school. If you were first chair tenor sax in high school, don't expect it at the college level unless you came from a great program.

This is no reason to be discouraged, but you should redouble your efforts. These can be a great break from class and encourage the development of the other sides of your life and personality. Before you get involved though, realistically look at the requirements of your schoolwork. If you have to work one or more jobs, are behind in your grades, and have to apply for med school in a year, you may have to take a break to get everything straight. You know yourself better than others and what your threshold is.

Black professional groups

These are some of the best resources you can have if you have any interest in a career aspiration. The most well-known are likely the National Society of Black Engineers (NSBE) and the National Medical Association (NMA). In addition, there are the National Bar Association (Legal), National Black MBA Association (NBMBAA), National Society of Black Physicists, National Organization of Black Chemists and Chemical Engineers, National Technical Association (science & engineering), Organization of African-American Linguists & College Language Association (linguistics), and the list goes on. If you are interested in any field, you should check to see if there is a Black professional organization, become a member, and if possible attend one of their annual conferences. They offer scholarships, career advice, networking, and even help you find if a certain career is for you. You can even start a chapter at your school or just be a member at large with the national organization. I find way too many people sleep on these groups until it's too late.

Being a leader

I always believe in made, not born, leaders, and college is the perfect place to hone your skills. You should definitely look at leadership roles, but how should you go about it? First, I would advise being a leader of only one or at most two organizations. To be effective takes a lot of time and effort outside of the general body meetings, and stretching yourself thin hurts you and the organization. Choose wisely and stick to what you chose.

I'm not an advocate for newcomers trying to become president so don't run for the highest spot at the first opportunity unless the group is brand new. To be an effective president, it helps to know how the organization works. In particular, running for a lower perch like secretary or finance is a much better starting point. That way you gain experience and credibility before moving ahead to a bigger position. Make sure you perform well in the lower role before asking for more responsibility.

As a leader you'll need to learn how to represent the group in the best light. You should also know any negative behavior on your part outside the group can still rub off on it. If you're president of the student council and are arrested for public drunkenness or rape, that will tarnish the organization whether you like it or not. We have enough public figures who can't manage their behavior. It may sound wrong to judge public figures by private conduct and I think in some cases the media goes overboard, but trust me, right or wrong, you and your organization will be judged. Conduct yourself according to the dignity of the position or don't run for it. It may be a harsh logic but it is good training for the real world where you can get away with much less.

In maintaining the group, there are two crucial factors: membership and finance. For any organization there is an iron rule of membership: if you do not gain more members than you lose, eventually the organization will cease to exist. Much earlier though the organization will become decrepit and ineffective. This does not mean you should necessarily strive for a huge organization. I've always believed a dozen committed people are more effective than a hundred apathetic people. Make sure you get feedback from members on what they want because their needs are what drives their non-compulsory participation in the club. Also, be aware that some people just don't care. When I was in school, a lot of Black organizations were frustrated because of the low meeting turnout and relative apathy of many of the Black students toward campus issues. You shouldn't expect every Black person to want to join or even empathize with Black organizations. Again, focused effort is better spent than casting a wide net to please everyone.

Members will have disputes and it's important to have a mechanism for resolving them without balkanizing the group. One thing you shouldn't do is take the grievance public or try to drive people out without proper consideration. Airing dirty laundry tends to attract onlookers, not make the laundry cleaner.

Finance is important because an organization's financial solvency enables or restricts its activities. First, whoever manages the finances, including the organization bank account, must be trustworthy.

Second, they should know basic accounting such as categorizing inflows and outflows of cash. They should also know how to invest the club money. A good option is to have working cash in a checking account with the surplus in a short-term, higher interest instrument like a CD or treasury bill with a six or twelve month maturity. Just know that pulling the money out early could entail penalties.

There must also be secure financial controls. For example, the finance officer who monitors the account should not be able to sign checks. Only the president or another officer should have signature authority. For added security, you can have checks that require dual signatures for cashing. Finally, the finance officer should report on the financial status of the organization monthly. He should also give recommendations for cutting unneeded costs or fundraising. A good source of funds is often the school, but you need to pay careful attention to eligibility requirements, application dates, and making sure club bylaws conform to school rules.

As a final note, you should mentor younger members of the organization. You won't be in school forever, and if the organization is to survive, you must gradually relinquish power and responsibility to the next generation, guiding them as you do. Holding on to all levers of power to the bitter end is immature and bad for the organization. By mentoring the next group, you ensure a bright future.

Extremist groups

We live in a time largely defined by fear as evidenced by the ongoing and seemingly eternal War on Terror. As part of this, many groups have fallen under the suspect or 'extremist' label whether or not they are malicious. This is possibly the largest such instance of group surveillance since the 1960s.

Unfortunately there's no clear definition of 'extremist'. Depending on the person and context it could be a racial supremacist group, anti-war group, drug legalization group, etc. The key is that given today's uncertain climate, some groups may unfortunately come under scrutiny.

New laws like the U.S. Patriot Act give the government wide electronic surveillance powers without obtaining a warrant. This is not to say you should be paranoid. However, if you take part in certain activities, such as mass demonstrations, you should realize you could end up in a file somewhere. Anti-war groups, the Occupy Wall Street movement, and others have attested to this fact. Always be cautious about with whom you associate and in what context. There are documents about a program formerly run out of the Pentagon during the Bush Administration called TALON, which invited tipsters to conduct surveillance of political activities and demonstrations near military installations.

What are the consequences? It's hard to say what if any there are unless you do something blatantly illegal. However, there can be situations where this could affect you via an unfriendly faculty member or administrator who knows of these activities. Be cognizant of such issues going forward, and if you have concerns, contact a lawyer or civil liberties organization such as the American Civil Liberties Union (ACLU) to know your rights.

Faith and spirituality

For many people, faith is an important part of their life. College can be a very challenging or enriching time in this regard. Challenging in that college, for all its great aspects, can have more than its share of temptation. Your mom isn't going to drag you out of bed on Sunday (or Friday or Saturday) to make you go to service. In fact, no one will really care. You can party all weekend and sleep until 2:00 P.M. and no one will stop you. However, it can be enriching in that there are new people and new opportunities to explore your current faith or the faiths of others.

Either way, college is a transition. It's where you may find out if your faith really means something, where your faith is challenged for the first time, or even where you lose one faith and pick up another—or lose faith altogether. The first rule is that you should guide your own religious habits. People may be more fervent than you or they may not care about religion. If you have a religious focus, you should look at how to maintain it.

One of the first things will be to find a local congregation. Typically this is a Christian church of some various denominations, or it could be a mosque or even a synagogue. There's often a campus chapel and this can be the quickest and easiest option. Talking to upperclassmen about where the best churches are near campus is often one of the best ways to figure this out. Then you find out service times and pick one to fit your schedule. If you go, it's best to be consistent. The reason being, going if you "feel like it" will, in the long-term, eventually mean not going at all. There will be exceptions, like Easter, but if the commitment is not there, they'll stay only exceptions.

Second, are you going to live a lifestyle that your religion requires? This can mean simple things like remembering Easter or doing something for the poor. For Muslims this can mean staying away from pork and alcohol. If there's a will, there's a way and though you're free to choose your own path, make sure it's your own decision and not one forced by peers or desire for acceptance. It also doesn't mean you have to be uptight all the time since you can still have fun like everyone else.

Probably the biggest challenges to most religious beliefs on campus tend to involve ethical decisions like cheating and premarital sex. Again, you'll have to do some soul searching to do the right thing but make sure it's your own decision, and not something you rationalize for convenience.

For those who want to get involved in church at a deeper level, community initiatives such as choir or ministry can be a good outlet. It can also help you get to know people in the wider community outside the university, something few people do. There are also campus-based groups such as Campus Crusade or associations for students who are Catholic, Muslim, or other religions to join and do projects.

One group that is typically left out of these discussions is non-believers such as agnostics or atheists. For many of them, college may be the first time they've ever met like-minded people. Secular humanist organizations are pretty active on most campuses and there exist Black-focused secular humanist groups. I encourage even the devout to read some articles or attend talks to at least hear their arguments and point of view. I would definitely condemn treating those who choose not to have a faith as pariahs or someone worthy of scorn. Let them follow their own path. You're not the gatekeeper of all truth.

If agnosticism or atheism is your bent, you should follow it and not pose for anyone else out of fear of acceptance. Granted, some people in this situation have been ostracized by religious families or communities and turn viciously on religion in college. Remember, everyone has a right to belief, and turning vitriol against those who may have once had it in for you is not a mark of maturity or freedom but rather insecurity. The strength of one's convictions and living a model life in the end stands out more than any amount of grandstanding.

The dangers of cults

Religion is one thing where I believe it's dangerous to be content as part of the sheep and just doing what everyone else does. Cults are a prime part of this danger. There is no widely accepted definition of a cult. Some people joke that a large cult is a religion and a small religion is a cult. I think there's some truth to this though that there are big differences between normal, positive religious expression and suspect organizations out there who in the name of spirituality try to smother their members' individualism and control their lives, relationships with the outside world, and even their connections with family. These kinds of cults are often active on university campuses for many reasons. First, there are many young and impressionable recruits who may be open to a message promising something new, different, and fulfilling. Second, despite having many people, campuses can be socially alienating for some and produce plenty of lonely souls needing comfort. Following this, college campuses have their share of despair for school and personal reasons and the absence of a well-defined family and community support network makes people very vulnerable. Finally, for some cults, campuses allow a pool of recruits who come from a respectable socioeconomic standing and could thus be good contributors.

Let me be clear, even mainstream religions or other organizations can have campus groups or orders that act a lot like cults. Some people, particularly those in the cult, will be offended if their faith is called by this name. Cults, regardless of affiliation, become dangerous for several reasons. Cults will attempt to dominate your thinking. You no longer think for yourself but rather judge your actions by exact adherence to the dogma of the cult, particularly from a charismatic leader. You could be cut off from friends and family as the cult tries to monopolize your time and demand that you contribute all free time to its events and people. It can be financially draining as exorbitant demands for contributions drain your bank account and adversely affect your finances. Cults can also be a risk to your health and well-being since some of their practices may involve extreme actions such as food and sleep deprivation, aberrant sexuality, or in extreme cases, death.

One of the biggest fallacies out there is that only idiots join cults. These groups attract some of the best and brightest since many people can rationalize away concerns if they have an overwhelming emotional need to belong. Some death cults such as Aum Shinrikyo who masterminded a nerve gas attack on the Tokyo Subway had members who had educations from top-tier schools. Don't think you're immune and the best way to stay out is not to play. There can be many ways to recognize a cult, but below are some of the warning signs I've gotten from experts who have studied this issue and people who have experienced it themselves. Granted, this can apply to any organization in part so you must take everything in context, but always listen to your gut to see if something is wrong.

1. There are two main ways people discover cults. One, there are advertisements or flyers for a meeting on a generally interesting topic, typically inviting those with open minds and often pushing some kind of secret wisdom or esoteric spirituality. Some just offer fellowship or community. Second, cult members can try to recruit you by inviting you to their meeting, worship service, etc. It can start innocently in talking about how good the members are and how you will be welcome. You must be careful because some of these groups know how to approach people who are emotionally precarious or have just had a setback in life—they need a friend and they will offer to be one.

2. At the meeting/service you are typically love bombed, which means you have lots of people come and welcome you and give you

an extraordinary, even over-the-top welcome. They'll welcome you into their lives
after knowing you for five minutes. They
may even offer help with your problems,
consolation, or in some circumstances, sex.
This is designed to create a quick emotional
bond and bring you into the organization.
Some cults can even employ devious tactics
such as drugs or psychological manipula-
tion to break down resistance.

3. The cult is often dominated by a central
figure who offers revelations, secret wisdom,
or community, but at a price. Sometimes an
idea or a larger organization takes the place
of a central leader. You must pay both in
money and time you must spend with the
cultists.

4. Inquiry and questioning of basic assumptions are not really valued, despite protesta-
tions to the contrary, and your questions
are dismissed, explained away, or told to be
kept quiet until later. Eventually the cult
starts to dominate your life, demanding
more of your time and in the worst case,
isolating you from your friends and family.
This could be a virtual isolation or physical
isolation at a compound or similar location.
By doing this, they can begin to mold your
views of reality and make your world view
congruent to that of the cult. In isolation,
there's no one to dispute their logic or practices.

5. Once you're a trusted member, you're told to recruit and the cycle begins again.

Again, one may object that some mainstream groups utilize some of these tactics in isolation. However, if they're practiced in combination with extreme insistence, the organization may be cult-like. Remember, cults can form not only around religious ideas but also political ones, economic theories, ethnic solidarity, common fears, etc. Keep on the lookout and remember, your true friends demand you think for yourself and make your own decisions.

Athletics

In this section, by athletics we mean those outside of the primary sports teams that people take up for their own growth and enjoyment. As mentioned in Chapter 5 on health, exercise is extremely important and most modern college campuses have many sources of athletic opportunity.

In particular, even if you don't play on the school team, there are often many intramurals on campus or in local area leagues in which you can participate. They range from basketball to kayaking, or just about any other sport. If you're looking for a sports team to join, remember, you don't have to restrict yourself to campus. The wider city, which some people shamefully never bother to go into, may have their own league which will give you options to play a larger group of people and expand your network.

Some intramural teams are well-funded and competitive and may travel to other schools to compete. The biggest downside to many intramural sports is that they have to be funded by the team or through fundraisers. If it's a campus organization it may get a disbursement of funds but otherwise, you need to assess the financial as well as time commitment, depending on how deep you want to get into it.

College is also a time to learn new sports, especially those with which you are not familiar. Before school I had little awareness of lacrosse or capoeira and you can become familiar with many of the rarer or new and up-and-coming sports or athletic fads at school. Remember, you will never be so young, in-shape, and have so much free time so it's an excellent opportunity to try new things.

Conclusion

College is the place for extracurriculars. You will never have so many opportunities, so I urge you to explore and broaden your horizons. However, it's easy to be overwhelmed, so balance your time so you can get the full participation from a few rather than dabble in many. This will make your participation and learning much more rewarding.

Chapter 7
Studying Abroad

It's a wonderful thing to have happened and the only other person I would have liked it to happen to is myself.
—James Baldwin

The quote above was from the famous expat writer, James Baldwin, while he was still living in the United States, to another famous writer and then an expat in Paris, Richard Wright. Baldwin described how he was happy Wright was enjoying Paris and Baldwin would soon arrive there himself.

Like Baldwin, if you are American and reading this, there is a high likelihood you have never left the States. There are many reasons for this, some of which are opportunity and cultural preferences ingrained in the psyche of Americans as a whole and many Blacks as well. I can't claim to have been much better since I never went abroad until I was twenty-two. The vast majority of U.S. citizens don't have a passport or speak a foreign language. Without the former, you aren't going anywhere, and without the latter the experience will not be as enjoyable. America is used to being the center of world power. It is a magnet for immigrants and has not typically exported people. How many Americans rely on remittances from relatives abroad to live? Not many, but much of the world does rely on these payments.

Americans also have a very skewed view of the outside world, often seeing it through the lens of news reports on war, disaster, famine, or stereo-typical movies. This can create a feeling that you are better and safer in the good old U.S. of A. In the Black community there can be another layer of this, which combines provincialism and a fear of the unknown with a fear that country X or Y may not be hospitable to Blacks.

I'm here to encourage you to cast these aside and plan on going abroad. Preferably this is to be done when you are young and not tied down with a family and expenses, so college is a great oppor-tunity. If not, planning to go by age twenty-five or before you're married is a good goal. The stats on Blacks studying abroad are unfortunately like many educational stats—lagging. According to the Institute of International Education though Black students are twelve percent of the U.S. college stu-dent population only about four percent of Ameri-cans studying abroad are Black. They're missing out on a lot and in this age of globalization, experi-ence abroad could have life-changing effects.

But enough talk, how does one prepare them-selves to go abroad. The first thing you must do is get a passport. The forms are free online, and though there is a fee and a need for a couple of photos, it's a painless process. It's a long process though so you should usually start long before you have to travel to avoid hefty expediting fees. Once this is done, you can start thinking of where to go.

As a student you have huge opportunities to go abroad for a semester, summer, whole year, or even just a vacation. With your student ID you will have access to numerous discounts the rest of the world does not and many students-only trips and travel services. In addition, you have logistical support from the school itself through the office for study abroad (otherwise known as overseas education).

Traveling abroad is a life-changing experience. There is no substitute for understanding the culture of other people without living it. In addition, you'll never have proficiency or fluency in any foreign language unless you're thrown into an immersion situation. Beyond the platitudes about experiencing other countries and cultures, there are other benefits as well. You'll learn how business works in other countries, and this could help you in your career. You can make lifelong friends who will be great to hold on to throughout the years. You will also make yourself more marketable to employers.

So, how do you go abroad? Once you have a passport in hand you need to figure out which countries to go to and for how long. If you are studying a foreign language, this can make your decision easier since you should aim for a country that speaks the language you are trying to become fluent in. Otherwise you should think of a country or region you would like to visit.

The best resource you have is your school's study abroad office. If you have even an inkling of studying abroad, you should attend their information sessions and pick up some brochures. If you're serious, you should set up an appointment with a member of the study abroad office to discuss options and get advice. Also, there are members of the foreign language or history departments at your school who can give valuable advice.

Another great resource is AAA (American Automobile Association), which has great travel advice and books. STA Travel, a student-focused travel firm, has offices near many college campuses, and their advice and travel help was great when I went to China for the first time.

If you're focused on a specific country or language, there are sometimes special institutes dedicated to study abroad. The Goethe Institutes and Confucius Institutes are dedicated to language learning and cultural understanding for students interested in Germany and China respectively. Other countries may have similar organizations. Finally, the embassies of many countries have an official dedicated to education or students studying in their country. Email or call this person, and there could be special help or scholarships to get you on your way.

Credits and scholarships

Before you go abroad, you need to make sure you know what credits you'll be getting and to make sure this will not affect your graduation time or ability to apply to any graduate schools. This is typically very easy depending on the program you choose, but make sure the study abroad office and your department major confirm this before you apply or pay any money. In some cases, you can make an argument a certain course should be counted as credit. By contacting the host institution abroad and getting a copy of the syllabus, you may be able to convince your department to count a course for credit, though it can be difficult.

Though study abroad is often cheaper than a normal semester, you should still search around for scholarships both at your school and through other organizations. Sometimes, taking a foreign language test administered by a foreign country can win you a scholarship. As an example, the HSK Chinese language test often gives scholarships to students to study in China. There are also organizations like the Association of African-American Linguists that offer scholarships for foreign language and study abroad.

Preparing to go abroad

Once you are set up to go abroad, there are a few things you should do. First, make sure your passport will not be expiring soon. Sometimes you cannot get into a country if your passport expires in less than six months. Second, make sure you have a visa if you need one for your destination country. Third, get any vaccinations the health clinic recommends. Typically you should get a tetanus booster, Hepatitis A and B, and maybe typhoid. For tropical regions, typically yellow fever and maybe malaria pills are required.

There are also other minor things to prepare such as figuring out whether you want to get an unlocked GSM cell phone, GSM is the most common cell phone system worldwide, or wait to buy one abroad. You should also let your bank and credit card companies know you will be abroad to prevent false alarms on the anti-fraud systems and let someone you trust know your personal and financial information in case of an emergency. Buy a security fanny pack, such as one you can wear under your shirt, if you're going to a country where petty theft may be common. You must also procure health insurance that is effective abroad. Your school's study abroad office or health clinic can help with this.

Learn something about the country you're going to besides basic tourist tips. For example, read a book about the country's history and start reading articles from a major newspaper from that country a few weeks before you leave. This familiarizes you with the past and present situation of the country and can help provide valuable context when you arrive. There are several basic things you should know about a country before you visit, including the capital city, the main languages and ethnic groups, the states/provinces/regions into which the country is divided (memorize them), major cities, common forms of transportation, and common etiquette. There are many forums and blogs by expats online that can give good advice. There is even a website for Blacks abroad called Black Expat (http://www.blackexpat.com). As a disclosure, I am a co-editor of the magazine.

Before leaving, it's also a good idea to register your contact information with the local American Embassy. If there's a dangerous natural disaster or political situation, the embassy can then contact you and advise on whether you should stay or leave. This registration can be done from the embassy or U.S. State Department web pages.

Being abroad

Going abroad is exciting, and you should take advantage of all opportunities that arise to learn about the country you're in. However, you should also remember some basic things. First, familiarize yourself with the area you stay in. Know which places are dangerous and which are not. If there's any question, ask a local you trust like a hotel desk person or someone at the university and they can let you know if a certain area is safe. These same contacts can also help you find the best places to hang out. If you're worried about being pickpocketed, only take one credit card, as much cash as you think you need, and a photocopy of your passport. Photocopies of passports are good since there is no fear of losing the real thing. Also, leave your cell phone in your pocket instead of on a clip if it is something savory to crooks like the latest iPhone.

You must be on your best behavior. I don't mean you have to be perfect or an angel, but you must realize that what you do will reflect on both your country and Black men in general. It's not fair, but all Americans who go abroad are indirect representatives of our country and must act accordingly or fall in the "ugly American" category. Likewise, if you display all the stereotypes of Black men, you'll make it harder for those who come after you. It's not right, and it may violate the ideas of individualism, but it's a reality you must always keep in mind.

If you go to a foreign country and just hang around people from your own or similar countries, you can miss out on valuable opportunities for intercultural communication and foreign language learning. If you want to learn the foreign language of the country you're in, stay away from the expat bars and English speakers and force yourself to use the language, even if you make embarrassing mistakes. This includes watching TV or listening to radio in the language in your free time, reading the non-English menu, and if possible, living in a part of town that has relatively few foreigners.

Making local friends also helps. It can be lonely at first but there are many ways you can meet people. The easiest is at the local school where you are studying or a job you may be fortunate enough to work at. You can also meet friends through common interests so you should try to join clubs and activities at the school or go to local events. If you have a focused interest such as a hobby, academic interest or type of art, you can look up local groups or people and contact them before or after you arrive in the country. I became friends with a professor when I was living in Beijing and he became a great friend and introduced me to many other people. Try to speak to them in the local language and not English if at all possible.

Always respect the local culture. Every local culture has things that may seem strange, but as long as it doesn't violate a moral precept, you should try to adapt. This is their country, and you owe it to them to at least try to understand the culture. Embrace local foods and search out local haunts. Often you may have a good meal that you can ask someone to teach you how to make. Don't eat at McDonald's or KFC every chance you get. The more effort you put into learning about the country, the richer your experience will be.

Finding a job abroad

If you love the country, its people, culture, and business opportunities, you may start thinking of staying long-term. This can be a daunting task, but it has been achieved by many and I urge you to seize any opportunity to work abroad while you are young—you won't regret it.

If you do want to work abroad, you need to focus on the key question any prospective employer will think about when they look at you: why should

I hire this guy versus a talented local employee or someone repatriating to their homeland after studying abroad? As the world has become more 'flat' as Thomas Friedman put it, the traditional advantages Americans had in business such as English proficiency, secondary education, and connections to other American companies are no longer huge differentiators. Every country has an increasingly more educated population, in places like Europe English is spoken by most people, and in places like China and India, more people are returning who left to pursue their education in the West but see better career opportunities in the land of their birth.

So what can you do? There are several keys to finding employment abroad.

1. Language skills. Though in many countries you can get by with only English, it would behoove you to start getting skilled in the local language and using it wherever possible. You are a lot less marketable if you have to drag a translator everywhere with you.

2. Know the requirements to get a work visa. Some countries like China are easy to stay in and work until a company sponsors you. Others like the European Union have stricter rules on work visas for foreigners making it harder for a company to legally hire you. You should know the best way to get a work authorization yourself since very few companies will want to hire a young college grad with little experience if they have to sponsor him.

3. Know the local economy. What parts of the economy are hot and what is driving them? This helps you gauge the best opportunities to search for employment.

4. American and maybe European firms may be easier to get in the door. Often, local firms may be reluctant to hire foreigners. A good first step is to look at local branches of American or European companies. Often, you can seek out lists of these companies and contacts through the local American Embassy or American Chamber of Commerce. Other countries have similar Chambers you can contact. Try to contact and set up a phone call or meeting with someone in a position you aspire to and ask them how to look for work in the country and what kinds of skills are necessary. You never know who may have an opening. Also join local expat clubs or mailing lists and go to parties and networking events.

5. Hone a skill. You must be good at something specific, not just a general major. You have to make a good pitch that you can contribute something they would otherwise not have. This could be English translation or teaching skills but also if you have job experience from internships or jobs back home that is valuable such as in IT or even hands-on skills like machining or electrical engineering.

Talking to women abroad

This is a common topic. I've traveled all over the world, and every time I come back to the U.S., at least before I was married, the guys would always ask how are the women? It's an honest question and one that's on many men's minds, though it's often unstated. Pitbull took that curiosity to a whole new level with his song *International Love*. Here's what I think is best, what to do and what not to do. I'll also try to dispel some myths of living in other countries.

1. Don't be the ugly American (foreigner)— This has already been mentioned but it needs additional reinforcement. Don't go over to another country acting like a clown or some sex-starved maniac. I've seen plenty of this, and it's interesting to see the local women smile and flirt but talk dirt about them in their native tongue. A lot of people think that being abroad means the rules don't apply. This is far from the case.

2. "Do they love Americans?"—There are certain countries where everyone says they love Americans. It's true that there are countries where Americans are more welcome and also can get a better reception from the locals. I'm always careful about the advice I hear though. Sometimes it's exaggerated and sometimes it's communicated by people who want to brag about their adventures rather than communicate real advice. Depending on where you go, Americans are foreign and exotic, and this can be an asset. I wouldn't rely on it though. I es-

pecially wouldn't say you should make it your persona. The bottom line is that if you have enough confidence you can talk to women in any country no matter where you're from.

3. "Do they love Black men?"—This is the second question. I've seen arguments between people about which countries are supposedly more welcoming to Black men. Granted, they often mean American Blacks since depending on where you are, your national origin may be more important than your color. Sometimes this leads to stupid stuff like what you see in Asia where some people try to act super Black to appeal to some segment of the local population who thinks all Blacks are in hip-hop or prison. This is also something that can vary on with whom you interact. People in bars are typically looking for a meet market and are not the standard for any population. A lot of people go to Roppungi in Tokyo and then get a mistaken idea about what Japan is really about.

4. Learn the language—Really, nothing endears you to locals in general more than learning the language, even if you don't speak well. I mean really learning and not just some phrase book sentences. Language helps open communication with more people and will expand your potential pool of friends and partners dramatically. There's probably no one better thing you can do to improve game and prospects abroad. I want

to tackle another thing I think is a myth, namely that having a foreign girlfriend will dramatically improve your language skills. If you already have learned some of the language and have an honest desire to learn more, having a girlfriend could help. However, I've seen more people start trying to learn and just lapse into English, if the girl speaks English, because it's easier. Also, depending on the tension in the relationship, some people get tired of their language mistakes being corrected and this can be an impediment to learning.

5. Make friends with...men—A lot of people laugh when I say this, but if you're in any foreign country, you should make guy friends. First, they're good pals to hang with, but second, there's no better way to meet a quality woman than to be introduced by a guy who knows and trusts you. I'm not a fan of bars and clubs and much prefer personal introduction and endorsement to the party scene. Even if they don't introduce you, they can tell you where to go, act as wingmen, and help screen out bad prospects. Take my advice, hang out with the guys, and you will meet the girls.

6. Be able to have interesting conversations—This goes with what I said earlier about learning about the history and current condition of a country. If you want bonus points, know the current popular songs and singers, read some literature, and maybe know some politics. If you can actually

have a real conversation about the country, it is a big plus and differentiates you from the mass of foreigners milling around.

7. Don't lie—Don't lie about you or your background. It's bad enough to lie to a girl to get with her, but it's insane to misrepresent your own background. A good example of this is the rock musical play, *Passing Strange* (available on DVD) where the protagonist talks about lying to his fellow artists in West Berlin about his background, claiming he was from a violent inner-city slum. He actually grew up middle class in Los Angeles. Lying always makes you look less genuine and why should you chase someone who doesn't like you for who you are anyway?

8. Be discriminating—Some men get so enamored with the attention they get from some women in foreign countries they forget common sense. As a man, you should pick who you want, not just grab whatever comes by. First, do you really think the best quality girls are the type to mob you just because they hear you're from a Western country or you're Black? How many times do you think they've done this to other men? Second, prostitution and scams are common in a lot of developing countries. When I was in Rio hanging with some Brazilians, they would point out how gullible Americans were who thought they were popular when the women surrounding them were all prostitutes. Also, I've talked to expats who

had stories of taking a woman home and waking up to find she had robbed him clean. Don't leave your common sense at home, and always keep your wits about you. Remember, if it's too good to be true, it probably is!

9. Be careful—Following from above, be careful. Don't follow girls into dangerous areas, and if you just met someone, don't let them tell you where to go with them alone. Nothing may happen, but they may be trying to scam you into buying high-priced drinks at a bar who hired them for this purpose, lure you to get robbed, or something similarly shady. Always stay in control. Also, if you don't know a girl well, don't bring her back to where you live. You don't even have to tell her your real name or where you live.

Conclusion

Studying abroad is a life-changing experience and one of the best decisions you can make. I encourage you to plan to study abroad at least a semester in college since there's no time when it will be as easy and when you'll have so few responsibilities. Open your mind and embrace the world.

Chapter 8
Transportation

I roamed through England, Scotland, and a bit of France in 1906 on a bicycle.
—W.E.B. DuBois on his travels in Europe

Our students are in earnest. One recently walked one hundred and seventy-five miles to reach the school in order that he might prepare himself to teach the people at his home.
—Booker T. Washington describing a student arriving at the Tuskegee Institute

So you need a ride. Maybe you are in a dense urban campus like Drexel University or a widespread more rural campus like Ohio State University. You're going to have to get from point A to B on and off campus, so you need to ride in style, right? Most of us won't have access to chick magnet sports cars or the latest sedan, but a car is a car and getting around doesn't have to be a social activity. But thinking even harder, what kind of car do you need, and do you even need a car? What are the expenses involved?

On the typical college campus, there are four or five dominant modes of transportation. There is the basic walking across campus, which takes time and isn't cool in bad weather. There are often buses run by the college to transport students across most common parts of campus. There are bicycles, which combine increased speed and flexibility, though are not the best for long distances. There are taxis, which more often than not are used if you are too drunk to drive or are going to the airport or bus station. Then there is the ultimate sign of adult attainment and virility: the car.

The Ride

Let's tackle the car first since this seems to be the holy grail of almost every college student. Cars are great. With no effort, you can get from point A to point B quickly, you can take girls on dates easily, and you can do those long-distance trips to the grocery or hardware store. On the other hand, parking is a pain and possibly expensive, gas isn't cheap, and the other costs do add up. Often, freshmen aren't allowed to have cars on campus for at least the first semester. This is both to teach them how to use the campus transportation and limit the number of cars the campus has to deal with. Before you bring a car on campus though, you need to account for costs.

First, you'll need a parking pass, which could be several hundred dollars per semester. Second, you have to keep up with regular oil changes and maintenance, including replacing tires or fixing problems. This can be less for a new car but it will still exist. Third, you must maintain your insurance to drive. As a male under the age of twenty-five, this is not a small sum. Fourth, you'll have to factor in the price of gas which is of course the most visible expense of driving. Finally, you have to deal with the aggravation of parking where space is often very limited.

Of these items, the parking pass and driver insurance are the easiest to predict. Parking permits can typically run several hundred dollars per semester or more depending on the location of the campus and school policies. Often, these permits cost more for off-campus residents than those on campus. Insurance for males under the age of twenty-five with no accident history can still vary by state, what kind of car you have, and even your grades. However, it will likely stay between $1,500 and $2,000 per year no matter what you do unless you roll the dice and increase your deductible amount.

So we are already likely at $3,000-plus per year for keeping a car on campus and we haven't even gotten to the car itself! For the other expenses, a good rule of thumb is the AAA guidelines from their *Your Driving Costs* study on the real cost per mile of driving your car. For sedans driven about 15,000 miles per year, the cost per mile including gas, tires, maintenance, and depreciation of the vehicle value can average fifty-nine cents a mile. For SUVs it jumps to seventy-five cents per mile. So for every 1,000 miles you drive, you are indirectly paying a minimum of about $600. These costs are uneven since oil changes, tire changes, and other maintenance are spread out over time. Also, this cost includes insurance, which we have already covered but given the cost estimate assumption is a middle-aged male with no accident history, it understates how much insurance you will actually have to pay. It also includes costs people usually don't consider such as depreciation, which is an implied cost by the decrease in vehicle value, vehicle registration, and periodic needed repairs.

Cars are a great help in college, but you need to account for the costs and pain too. I'm not trying to discourage you from having a car in college, but you should be cognizant of the added costs you'll be paying. If gas goes higher due to global shortage or a war in the Middle East, these figures will get even starker. One of the biggest questions to ask before you bring the car on campus is what are you going to use it for? If you are commuting home often, the cost can be worth it if there are no other good options like Amtrak or the bus. However, if it's just a feeling of freedom, going to the grocery store, or going on dates, you need to evaluate if the cost is worth it. One way to figure it out is using your work-study, campus job, or previous summer job as a benchmark. With your hourly rate, how many hours are you working to sustain your car on campus? If you make a net salary of ten dollars an hour, you'll be working at least two hundred hours to cover your car expenses. If you have a ten-hour work week, this can be almost half the school year. If you make twenty dollars an hour, the figure is half as much time, but the same logic applies. Think of what you use your car for and whether you would work that many hours to have that benefit? If not, what do you do? There are a few alternatives to still get access to a car.

Mooching a ride is one time tested practice. If it's something like grocery shopping, you usually will have a friend who can offer you a ride if they're going in the same direction. Abusing this privilege is not looked on highly though. It's also possible for multiple people to share a car, but there has to be a good honor system on who gets access to the car and when, who pays for gas and maintenance, etc.

A newer addition is the ZipCar option. ZipCar is like the Netflix of car rental. Instead of a fixed period like with a regular car rental you join the service and can reserve a ZipCar for any time and place you want though you have to be at least twenty-one years of age. ZipCar has a service at some schools that allows you to circumvent the twenty-one and older restriction. This is a more recent option but you can weigh this as a way to have the convenience of a car without owning it outright if the service is available in your area.

Traditional car rentals typically have an age minimum of twenty-five though some like Enterprise allow younger people to rent with a surcharge. I have never seen this as an economical long-term solution though.

Driving Safety

If you own a car, it is essential that you understand driving safety, defensive driving, and basic car maintenance. Defensive driving courses not only keep you safe, for example understanding blind spots around tractor trailers, but can reduce your insurance premium. Also, if you are moving farther north for college, it is essential you learn how to drive in snow and ice and also how to buy snow tires.

Basic car maintenance includes checking oil, coolant, and other fluids at least once a week and checking tire pressure and tread wear at least once a month. Know the correct pressure for your tires and replace tires whenever treads get low at around 3/32" or 4/32". Do not wait until the legal limit of 2/32" since you are in danger of skidding in bad weather. Tire pressure and tread gauges cost about $5 each. Finally, if your car has a recommended maintenance schedule, adhere to it. An ounce of prevention is worth a pound of cure.

Living without a ride...it is possible!

From the outset, I'll tell you much of this advice is from personal experience since I didn't have a car at any time during college. It can be done and you can still live just as functional a life. So what are your options?

The bike

Mass bicycling and college are almost synonymous. Bikes have several advantages. One, they give you the independence of not relying on school transportation or a car for short-to medium-range trips. Second, they're an excellent source of exercise and keep you healthy. Finally, they're extremely cheap to maintain, and a good bike can take a lot of crap.

My bike got me around campus for my latter three years, and I think it was one of the best decisions I made. I never had to wait on the often late school bus again to make it to class. I could take shortcuts. I also had somewhere to park. Finally, it helped keep me in shape. Of course, there are downsides. Inclement weather such as heavy rain, snow, or ice is bad news for bikers. There are also a myriad of safety issues you have to be very careful about. Bikes are primarily modes of transportation and not about looking cool. You should wear a good sports helmet—these can be had for under fifty dollars—with the Consumer Products Safety Commission (CPSC) certification. Also, you should have reflectors and lights on the front and rear of the bike. Typically for night travel, you want a steady white light on the front and a flashing red light in the back. Don't rely only on the light though, and try to wear lighter clothing at night or put on a reflective vest over your clothes so you are seen by drivers.

Bikes are also frequent targets of theft, especially if they're new with all the bells and whistles. You need to invest in a good bike lock—not just some chain from the hardware store any chump can cut off in a second. Most recommended are U-locks, which are defined by their shape. There are some modern chain locks that are appropriate but you should look at online reviews from *Consumer Reports* or another source to verify their quality. Also, register your bike with campus police and/or local law enforcement so if it's ever stolen and recovered, they can trace it back to you. Finally, always remember to lock your bike using the frame and not the wheel. The wheel can easily be removed and the rest of the bike stolen if you lock using the wheel.

Keep aware of your surroundings. Don't assume cars will stop, even if you have the right-of-way, and never pass a car trying to execute a turn. When you're turning, always use your hand to indicate the direction. Yeah, it may look dorky but it's preferable to lying paralyzed on the pavement. I don't support listening to music on bikes either for a similar reason. Keeping safe requires being aware of your environment. The bike ride is usually only a few minutes. Lil Wayne can wait until you reach your destination.

Bikes can do things people don't usually think about. You can add a basket to carry supplies like groceries. This is much better than the balance-plastic-bags-on-handlebars method (yes, I tried that). If you're in shape, which is likely the case after riding a bike for a bit, the hills aren't that big a deterrent either.

In buying a bike, you should look at what you need, not what the store wants to sell you. You do not need a full-suspension mountain bike for campus. I liked the front suspension mountain bikes and that's what I used through school, but you would be just fine with a typical road bike. Just look at your price point, style, brand quality, and you will likely not go wrong.

School transit

Most schools tend to have some form of transit now. Typically these are buses that follow fixed routes on and off campus. These are probably the most popular form of transit and are free. Their on-time performance can vary but are a good default option. The biggest issue is if you miss the bus, you may have to wait for another ten minutes, so hopefully you weren't in a rush to your midterm. If you can't find a stop nearby where you want to go, you have to walk the rest of the way.

Another option that is frequently underutilized are the night-time shuttles or similar transit services that act as a sort of on-campus taxi so students don't have to walk home alone at night. These can be a good option after a long and tiring study session at a library halfway across campus.

Mass transit

If you're in a major city or even medium-sized town, public mass transit becomes an option. In places like New York City or Boston, this is vital. In smaller towns, it may not be useful. You should at least evaluate the mass transit map when you get to school. It may go to useful places and will come in handy every now and then. You should always know where you're going though, and if unsure, ask the bus driver if you're on the right bus to your destination. Major cities also have trip planner websites that can help you find the exact route needed to go to your destination.

You can also ask the locals about an area if you've never gone there, are unsure of the location, or safety. The best thing to do is to call your destination and ask for advice since that could help you find the best way in any case.

Intercity transit - buses and trains

Depending on where you are, intercity transit by bus or train can be an attractive opportunity. Amtrak can be a good deal if you get tickets early enough, and it's a comfortable ride with electric sockets and sometimes Wi-Fi for computers. Amtrak can be much more expensive on the Eastern seaboard though.

Buses have improved over the years. Greyhound has made many service and equipment improvements to get rid of its reputation as a shady form of transportation with dodgy passengers. The Bolt buses on the East Coast compete with MegaBus and other options for super cheap transportation if you order a couple of weeks in advance. In many towns, there are the Chinatown buses that offer cheap transportation between cities, though it is first-come, first-served in cash payments. The East or West coasts can allow many options for traveling without touching an airport. If you use these often, you may want to join AAA since you can often get special discounts on fares.

Taxis

Depending on where you are, it can be easy to hail a cab or you may have to keep the phone number handy to call when needed. I was able to find one cabbie with whom I became friends with and regularly called every time I needed to go to the airport. Just be sure to call early during peak times like holidays or the end of the semester. Otherwise the cab companies quickly become saturated with other riders and may not be able to pick you up at your preferred time.

Walking

Is walking really that bad? Some people at college act like it's a violation of human rights to make them walk more than twenty feet. It may not be a preferred mode of transportation at all times, but sometimes waiting for a ride takes twice as long as the walk would have taken. Listen to Mrs. Obama and move.

Conclusion

Getting around in college isn't complicated but you should weigh carefully whether a car, bike, or just the bus is good enough for you. Expenses and flexibility need to play a part in your budgeting and decision making.

Chapter 9
Race and Class

*If you find a disputant while he is hot, and if he
is superior to you in ability, lower the hands,
bend the back, do not get into a passion with him.
As he will not let you destroy his words, it is utter-
ly wrong to interrupt him; that proclaims that
you are incapable of keeping yourself calm, when
you are contradicted. If then you have to do with
a disputant while he is hot, imitate one who does
not stir. You have the advantage over him if you
keep silence when he is uttering evil words. "The
better of the two is he who is impassive" say the
bystanders, and you are right in the opinion of
the great.*

*If you find a disputant while he is hot, do not des-
pise him because you are not of the same opinion.
Be not angry against him when he is wrong;
away with such a thing. He fights against himself;
require him not further to flatter your feelings.
Do not amuse yourself with the spectacle which
you have before you; it is odious, it is mean, it is
the part of a despicable soul so to do. As soon as
you let yourself be moved by your feelings, com-
bat this desire as a thing that is reproved by the
great.*
—The Precepts of Ptah-Hotep, a book written in
Ancient Egypt around 2200 BCE

Race and class issues are omnipresent on many
campuses. Even if there's no seeming tension, it

can always lurk beneath the surface. While we cannot always control what happens, we can control our responses. An intelligent and reasoned response is always much more effective than an emotional outburst or worse, vandalism or violence. These types of heated reactions are not rare; race and class are some of the biggest fault lines that can exist on campuses. This chapter will discuss common issues, first of race and then class. It will also discuss how to respond, and sometimes more importantly, how not to respond.

Racial commentary

Campuses can be a hotbed of racial commentary. There can be comments by students, professors, publications or organizations, university officials, or guest speakers. There can be many types of incidents. Some are completely innocent and due to someone not knowing that a term or activity is offensive. I didn't know Irish Americans found the term 'paddy' derogatory until a college friend of mine corrected me. There can be similar mistakes by those who did not grow up around Blacks and have a skewed frame of reference as to what is acceptable.

Other comments can be intentionally controversial but possibly within bounds. This often happens when talking about political topics. The person isn't trying to be offensive just to offend but to communicate a political point. There can be various ways to respond and keep the conversation in safe territory.

Finally, there are comments that are intentionally inflammatory. These are made by people to communicate a certain view or invoke a certain response. You will likely run into these unless you're at an HBCU, though historically Black colleges can have volatile debates on racism and colorism too. It is critical that you respond, even if defensively, in the correct way to such challenges.

In your daily interaction you may run into comments that may provoke a reaction. Some people may say something disparaging or racist. Often, it's more implied than outright calling someone a nigger. How you respond to these can be crucial to both keeping the high ground as well as dispel any incorrect notions. Most of your interactions will be with fellow students, and here is where most conflicts originate. If faced with a situation, be it a verbal insult or an overheard comment you should keep everything in context. There is nothing, including being called a nigger, that is worth a reaction that will get you kicked out of school, otherwise harm your education, or worse go to jail. When someone directs a comment such as this toward you I have several favored responses.

First, say nothing or just acknowledge them and walk away. This may seem like punking out or weakness but gauge the situation correctly. Does anyone who insults you in such a manner really care about your response? Or are they just trying to provoke you? Walking away from such a comment, I have found, often leaves the abuser awkward and diminished in front of onlookers. Your pride may be hurt and seared, but you took the high ground and dismissed the incident. This was a response also outlined by Ben Carson in his book *Gifted Hands*.

The second way is to ask someone to explain themselves. They may have uttered a comment that packs an emotional punch but has very little substance behind it. Unless you respond emotionally and escalate the situation, they are vulnerable. If they want to accuse you of something like being a quota or call you a name, force them to back up their assertions. You don't owe them a response, they started it. At the end you can ask if their comment applies to you or if the person is just venting. At this point they will typically walk away (or be pulled away by friends) or if desperate try to escalate things—a tactic for which you should never fall. There may be some people who don't know they are being offensive, for example by using words like 'going ape'. In these cases, don't make a scene but maybe approach the person in a friendly manner and let them know a lot of people (including you) don't think such a comment is cool. By not publicly embarrassing them and handling it coolly, you can correct the error and maybe make a friend.

One situation you must always be careful around is one where alcohol is involved. People have fewer inhibitions and may say or do things they would not otherwise. It's often best to walk away from situations with alcohol since the person isn't thinking or reasoning clearly, and it is easy for events to escalate into violence.

Political conversations or commentary on society are a more mixed bag. These come from students, especially representing political groups or newspapers, and professors. On one hand, someone has a right to oppose affirmative action, inner-city crime, and argue for stiff penalties for crack cocaine. There's a way to express these arguments in an objective manner though without intentional jabs. When you're in this situation, especially in a classroom, the most dignified and effective way of dealing with this is to address the argument head-on. You should make an effort to be well read on many political and social issues that boil over on campus and know the facts. Know the difference between credible factual sources, sources with little credibility, and anecdotal evidence. The first way to challenge a statement is to address the sources of their data. Is this an absolutely unequivocal result or is it based on a limited set of biased research?

Next, if you're well-researched, interject a countering view. Never attack the person as an individual and always stay above board. As stated in Chapter 2 on academics, never embarrass or insult a professor. You can politely disagree with them in class and it is often effective to ask a rhetorical question or challenge them to validate one of their assumptions rather than attacking them personally. If you have beef with them, take it up in their office hours personally. You can often resolve things with professors you disagree with without a crowd, which makes both people scared to back down. You should always talk to a professor first before going to the university administrators. It is usually difficult to force the administration to discipline a tenured professor, and the professor may seek vengeance through grades or blacklisting you. The thing is you may not win and convince them, but countering the argument will make them respect you and give a different perspective to listeners.

Often, there may be editorials in a school newspaper that will take a controversial or offensive stance toward Blacks. Again, it's best to deal with these in a mature manner. Fight fire with fire and ask the newspaper if they will allow you or someone else eloquent to write a counter editorial. Some professors may give good guidance on what to write and facts to include. You may even approach professors or scholars in other universities or organizations for material and support. In these very public cases, it's important to have a response to correct such egregious errors. Always use facts where possible that undermine the argument rather than appealing just to fair play or readers' emotions. Attacking the writer of the editorial is rarely a good idea. It changes nothing and allows the writer to, sometimes disingenuously, declare themselves a martyr for the cause of free speech and free expression. This shifts the argument from the errors of their writing to a greater—and much agreed—value such as free speech. In these situations it's easy to look like the bad guy so you should avoid personal attacks even if you don't like or respect the character of the writing.

Closely related are guest speakers. Many campus organizations will invite controversial speakers. These events will be well advertised with teasers to attract a large number of the student body. The speaker may then more or less attack Blacks, civil rights, or anything related. Sometimes they do so to count on an adverse reaction by Black students, which again lets them claim they are "purveyors of the difficult truth" and being persecuted by politically correct Blacks because of their views. This is a common tactic, and sometimes they will use anecdotes of unruly Black students or even photos to show they are being persecuted for their beliefs. Many hot heads unintentionally hurt their own cause by acting unruly, attacking speakers with nonsensical questions, or acting in a manner that is viewed by other students as disruptive.

Again, no response is better than a non-reasoned response. If a controversial speaker is coming, you can look them up online and perhaps contact people who have debated or criticized them before. This will give you useful questions to ask during the session. In addition, ask your fellow students to not get out of hand in a way that will just give the speaker ammunition. Really, some people thrive on anger directed at them. Following the speaker, writing editorials for the paper or bringing a counter speaker are useful tactics.

The worst incidents are altercations that involve conflict and violence. If these occur, first do your best to diffuse it, but otherwise don't get involved. Calling the authorities is better than duking it out. When the authorities eventually arrive, you all may be arrested, but as a Black male the book could get thrown at you harder. Again, realize you are in school for a reason. Your ancestors would be more satisfied to see you back out of a fight and get your degree than defend your honor and end up expelled. I'm not advocating weakness, but you should always control a conflict. You should fight at the time and place of your choosing and by the (nonviolent) methods that best suit you. Being pulled into situations opposes this basic rule.

When such incidents do occur, make sure you contact the university administration to ask for guidance. Such incidents should be dealt with by both the university and local law enforcement. Whenever you have difficulties with law enforcement, follow the ACLU guide from Chapter 5 on health and safety. Never confront the officer, just get out of the situation and find your options for legal recourse later.

Dealing with all of these, the important thing to do is educate yourself. You should know about the basic social and political issues, especially those involving race, and learn how to respond to arguments. Educational quotas have been illegal for thirty years since Bakke v. Regents of the University of California. But people still bring them up as if this is being used anywhere. Also, know about your university's policies so that you can better attack or defend them. Knowledge always trumps any amount of bluster and a well-stated argument is better than ten loud outbursts. Keep your knowledge up to date, and you should be able to handle many of these challenges.

Class issues

Class issues cut across ethnic groups. There can be class issues with Blacks and non-Blacks, but here we'll focus mostly on intra-Black class issues. There's a widening class gap in the Black community. While I still think the class divisions within Blacks are not as bad and blatant as in other communities, they do exist and seem to be growing. The basic egalitarian nature of the university means that a person who grew up skiing every winter in Utah and someone who is the first of their family to go to college will be in some of the same social circles. Granted, cliques can eventually form that will tear them apart but the interaction is still frequent.

There can be affronts from both sides. Some people from more privileged backgrounds may look down at other Blacks from "ghetto" or single-parent backgrounds as less than suitable friends or dating material. It may not matter what your education or smarts are, to them you are just not bourgeoisie. On the other hand, less privileged people can be cruel as well. For example, I know two girls who talked bad about another girl because despite the fact they were all from Chicago, she was from an affluent suburb and they grew up on the South Side. She just wasn't "real" to them or was seen as somehow less Black.

Class identities can tend to make people on some campuses feel ostracized or unworthy. The background of many colleges is solidly middle class or upper middle class. A student of limited means who cannot afford the clothes, shoes, cars, or any other status symbol may feel left out. Luckily, for men this feeling of isolation is usually not as acute as it is for women. After all, when is the last time someone cared what designer brand your wallet is? It can have an impact, however, both in interactions with peers and the opposite sex. Some people deal with this by withdrawing from social life or choosing other peer groups. I would encourage you to choose peers who don't judge you based on materialism but don't ostracize yourself. You never know where people will go in the future, and it helps to be on good terms with them. Others try to pose. For some this means living way beyond their means using credit cards to buy themselves a certain status. This eventually ends in financial disaster.

Another way of coping is that some middle class students will pose as a thug in order to make themselves seem more real or authentic. This sends the wrong sort of signals to your peers and yourself. You should never have to pose to fit in, and you should examine your idea of Blackness if you think it dictates migrating toward a thug persona.

Class issues can also mix with race issues. For example, some people will blithely look down on poor or rural Whites and use the terms 'white trash' or 'trailer trash' with ease, seemingly oblivious to the pain they would feel if Whites referred to 'ghetto blacks' in a similar manner. Don't be so insensitive and make yourself think that somehow looking down on someone because of class is more ok if it is across the color line. Always put yourself in the same position and imagine if Whites referred to any Blacks in a similar fashion.

Dealing with class issues can sour your college experience if you let it. It can also help you choose friends better by understanding early on who is superficial and who isn't. There is nothing to be ashamed of having grown up poor, and you don't have to prove your Blackness if you grew up middle class. Holding adversarial or disparaging views toward another class never helps anyone in the end and only serves to highlight your own fears and insecurities. Choosing your peer group only by class or race is not a good idea. Make sure your friends have character and you'll find you'll spend much more time having fun than worrying about the perceptions of others.

A final issue that often raises its head in the Black community is that of male/female relations. While class issues in the Black community may be less contentious than other groups, I think the battle of the sexes is worse. There seems to be an almost adversarial relationship sometimes between Black men and women on campus, which is sad. Given that women are now the majority on most campuses, sometimes this can take the view of women looking down on men despite the historical trend of the opposite. I remember once arguing at school with a Black freshman woman about the Black female/male ratio at the University of Virginia. She said it was seven to one. Her friend said she was wrong and it was ten to one. I went to the registrar and requested the actual data. There were more women but it was only three to two. No, the athletes weren't the majority either. Much of the ratio was made up by the huge Black male majority in the engineering school. I gave this to someone who was holding a Black woman's summit on campus. She told me afterward that people had told her she was a blatant liar and the statistics were false.

Moral of the story is sometimes we can believe the worst about ourselves and each other more than anyone else. It's easier for Black men to disparage Black women as gold diggers or ghetto, and it's easier for Black women to invent ridiculous disparity numbers to justify either their own achievement or why they're currently single. In the end, it doesn't help anyone. Much of what I believe about this was discussed in the Chapter 4. If a White person said half the less-than-factual stuff we say about one another, we'd call them racist and pull out research statistics to refute them. When we say it among ourselves people just nod and accept it. I know the Black community has issues; you know it too. However, creating our own internal frictions over stupid exaggerations isn't going to help solve anyone's problem or make anyone more accepted. Treat our sisters with dignity and ask only that they do the same.

Conclusion

You're at the college of your choice and you deserve to be there no matter what people may say about your background. Granted, now you have to academically prove yourself to succeed in college, but that's something everyone faces. Responding to challenges in college is as much about keeping a cool head and being knowledgeable as well as passionate. Do these things and you'll not only survive the challenges, you'll emerge from them stronger.

Chapter 10
Technology

Learn about hardware as well as software.
—Marc Hannah, Co-founder Silicon Graphics

But if we're not plugged in, we can't play. And if we don't play, we can't expect to win.
—Carolyn Brown, Techwatch Editor, Black Enterprise Magazine (2000)

A lot of us come from different starting places when it comes to technology. For some, the computer they get for college will be the first one they've ever had. Hopefully it won't be the first they've ever used. Some will be proficient in all the neat gadgets like iPads and smartphones in addition to basic computer knowledge. Some will come in with a background of hardcore programming in C++, Java, or even assembly language. There's no denying, however, that college is a tech mecca like no other.

College is a convergence of skills, knowledge, hardware, and high speed Internet access that makes many of the most outlandish and faddish computer techniques commonplace. It's definitely the best place to enhance your computer skills and pick up new ones. Technology is not only wonderful, these days it is essential. One of the biggest problems though is some people are afraid of or uncomfortable around technology. This is usually due to a lack of knowledge. This deficit should be confronted head on, not hidden away due to embarrassment. In one semester, you can go from knowing almost nothing to knowing more than ninety-five percent of Americans. Really.

First, you need to honestly assess your level of techno-savvy. Below are some general levels I've seen many people fit into. Where do you fit on this continuum?

> Technophobe—Can't type well but can use a mouse. You are really not comfortable around computers.

> Getting by—Can type and do basic operations in Windows or Mac but not much else.

> Regular User—Skilled in computer usage and popular applications (Microsoft Office) and can fix basic technical problems like antivirus and system restore.

> Private Geek, First Class—Basic knowledge of programming in a major programming language, understands the basics of computer functions, can fix or find out how to fix major issues; may use Linux.

> Proud Nerd—Advanced programming knowledge and knowledge of detailed computer and network issues and functions. Perhaps some hacking skills.

It doesn't matter where you start; there is always room to learn. However, if you haven't gotten to at least the Regular User level after your first year in college, you're setting yourself up for academic and professional difficulty. Being there after your first semester is the best case scenario. Most of this chapter is dedicated to those with knowledge from Technophobes to Regular Users. College and the work world are very much information technology (IT) dependent and this trend is only accelerating. Knowing IT and how to use the campus network and resources is essential to your coursework where you often have to get material and submit assignments online. If you aren't there yet and need help, this should be a top priority.

There are various ways to get help. If you know you need it, you should start before you get to school. First are books. There are a lot of book series such as the *Dummies* series, etc., but my favorite was the *Busy People* series though it has been discontinued. If you feel your knowledge of computers is poor I'd recommend you get at least three books: one for Windows/Mac, one about the Internet (*The Internet for Busy People* is great), and one about the Microsoft Office products, which is the most common word processing/spreadsheet/presentation package.

Is your typing poor? Do you have to look at the keyboard and peck at the keys? You should definitely get Mavis Beacon Typing or a similar package. College will be hard enough without you typing your papers half as fast as your classmates because of a lack of practice. In addition, there are likely classes offered by the college or its IT department on computer fundamentals. If you have doubts, definitely attend. Finally, some of the best sources for help are computer savvy dorm mates or friends. They can help walk you through specific questions and issues. Some may be overbearing or arrogant, but it's definitely a benefit to find one who's happy to help.

Buying a computer

For at least a decade, a computer has been a required item at school. In my day, most had desktops and none but a fortunate few had laptops. Wi-Fi was not yet widespread so laptops had a limited utility. Now multiple devices are often common. There are people who now go to college with a desktop, laptop, and tablet computer. Some schools require laptops and others are now offering iPad-compatible textbooks. At the very minimum, I would recommend purchasing a laptop. Next, I would recommend a desktop. If you're looking for basic performance, you can probably get both for a combined price of under $1,500.

Desktops can be more powerful, however, and I would recommend buying a medium-to-high powered one for your room. This is primarily what you'll use to play games, watch movies, and probably do other increasingly power-hungry applications. In this situation, you would want at least the latest mid-range to high end processor as well as a high end graphics accelerator. At press time, the most famous examples of these are the Intel i5 or i7. Granted, you don't have to get the highest end but it's best to buy a computer that can keep you in good stead for four years. Moore's Law, the industry standard that states computer processor power doubles every 18 months, dictates that by the time you graduate in four years, computers will be at least six times faster. So pay the fifteen hundred dollars for a good laptop and desktop and it will keep you satisfied throughout college. If finance is an issue, I would get a lower end laptop since their power is limited and you will in all likelihood not be using it for anything more powerful than doing class assignments and watching movies. Memory wise I would recommend at least eight gigabytes of RAM in both units and a hard drive of at least one terabyte in a desktop or five hundred gigabytes in a laptop. Note these are mid-2012 numbers, so in the future upgrade them accordingly.

Brand is not as huge an issue now as in the past. If you're not getting a Mac, you can do well with Dell, HP, Lenovo, Samsung, Sony, Toshiba, and more. If you're looking for reviews, websites like CNET and PC Magazine have many very valuable reviews. Internet searches can also show discussion threads that talk about the various models, processors, options, etc. Just know what you want, and don't allow yourself to be sold on a bunch of options you don't need and won't use.

In addition to computers, there are also many valuable peripherals. First, you need a good set of speakers—though you'll likely have a roommate and neighbors so you don't need something that will blow the windows out. A good set of speakers can easily be had for less than fifty dollars as long as you aren't looking for high-end audio. Next, you need a printer. Preferably this will be at least a printer with a scanner that is Wi-Fi enabled. Copy and fax are also important though not as critical to have in your room. The best case would be a printer/scanner/copy/fax module with Wi-Fi support. Inkjets are fine though some prefer laser. Again, your price range and needs will dictate what you buy. Remember though that the majority of printer ownership costs are not the printer itself. Buying ink and paper over the long term will cost you far more so make sure you analyze the relative ink costs of each model before you buy. Search for printing costs per page for your printer online to see how it compares. Surprisingly, the cheaper the printer, the more it usually costs per page in ink so you may save over the long-term by spending a bit more upfront on the printer to save ink costs. Also, paper can cost between half a cent to one cent per sheet so this allows you to calculate the costs of owning the printer. A good exercise is to divide the printer cost by the print cost per page to see how many pages you have to print to equal the cost of the printer. If the printer costs $150 and has a $0.10/page cost to print, after 1,500 pages you have already bought another printer! This may seem like a lot of pages but it is only three reams of printer paper.

For public printers, campuses are now charging more and more for printing. Usually you get allo-cated a certain number of pages free each semester and afterward you pay between five and ten cents per page. This may or may not be more economical than your home printer since the school buys ink, toner, and paper in bulk. If it is cheaper per page than your home printer, you can save money on large print jobs by just paying for it at the library or computer lab. It's hard to believe I could once print at the computer lab for free! There are other peripherals that may or may not be included with your computer, like microphone headsets for Skype or webcams. Sometimes, these are already bundled with a desktop or built into a laptop. The-se are best purchased via mail order since store prices are usually a rip-off. Same goes with Ether-net, USB, and HDMI cables. Some well-known online stores like Amazon or off-the-beaten path sources like MPJA.com and Jameco.com put the prices of the major chains to shame.

Software

Now that you have the hardware, you need to put it to good use. Software is what people understand better and there is a huge variety. The first piece of software, already on your computer, is the operating system. This system, such as Linux, Windows, or Mac OS, provides the interface for other software with the computer hardware. Typically it is Windows or Mac OS depending on what you buy. College can be a great time to explore Linux though. Linux is the free, open-source operating system that is frequently used by computer enthusiasts for its security, ease of use, and many features. It is also more stable than Windows and has a huge library of free software for most common applications. There are many distributions, however, asking the IT department or someone in the know can help you see which one is right for you. If you are dedicated to learning it and don't feel a need for specialized software only on Windows or Mac, Linux can be a great choice. However, if you are just worried about common applications or playing games (often not available on Linux) and don't want to have to learn a new operating system, Linux may not be for you.

Next are what are called "office productivity" software packages, usually the Microsoft Office suite. This should at minimum include Microsoft Word, a word processing program good for typing anything from papers to books, Microsoft Excel, a spreadsheet program used to organize data for calculations such as in lab reports, and Microsoft

Powerpoint, a presentation software package to create slide shows that is used throughout school and the work world. Microsoft Access, a database program, is good if you need something to handle large amounts of data but for the ordinary user, the latest versions of Microsoft Excel have made Access less of a necessity for large amounts of data. Microsoft Visio is a flow chart design program but this is more specialized and you can typically get by with it from the school computer lab instead of buying it. These can often be bought with your computer at the time of sale for several hundred dollars. If this gives you sticker shock though, you have other options.

In particular, there is a free office productivity suite called OpenOffice that can allow you to open Microsoft Office files and save in their format. It can lack some specialized features of the Microsoft products but it can be a great alternative to try. There are other free office productivity packages such as LibreOffice though I don't have direct experience with them. If they don't meet your needs, you haven't wasted any money and you can upgrade to Microsoft Office later.

Next are computer security packages. These will be discussed more in the section on computer security in this chapter but you need to have an antivirus program installed and keep it updated throughout college. Computer viruses and hackers are only getting more sophisticated so you need to stay safe online.

Probably the most used software on computers now are web browsers. Web browsers always come with Windows (Internet Explorer) or Mac (Safari) computers. In addition, there are several free alternatives though which you may want to try. Mozilla Firefox, Opera, and Google Chrome are the most well-known and all three function great. My personal favorite is Firefox given its privacy features and huge library of add-ons that can enhance browser functionality. New versions are coming out all the time so check reviews online and see which browser features the best speed, functionality, and website compatibility.

Games need no introduction and are the craze on any college campus. If you are a hardcore gamer, I would recommend spending more money on your computer to get the best possible processor and graphics support. Games get more powerful all the time so you need a high end PC to play them correctly, especially with multiplayer games online.

There are many other types of software out there but before you buy something expensive, check to see if a free, open-source version is available. A lot of laboratory graphs and computing is done with R or Octave, great graphics and illustration can be done with GIMP, and most programming languages now have good free compilers. If in doubt, use the computers at the library for expensive software packages that the college might subscribe to. Remember, there is no rush and you can always buy it later. If you do buy it, however, always ask to make sure there is a student discount or student version you can buy. These are typically much cheaper.

College computer networks

One of the most ubiquitous and important resources in college is the computer network. It gives you high-speed access via Ethernet cable or Wi-Fi virtually anywhere on campus. For many, the campus network is pretty much just something you plug in to use Google. However, it is much deeper and more complex.

The campus network is your most ubiquitous method of connecting to the Internet, and it helps to be familiar with it. Beyond Internet access there are several services the campus will undoubtedly offer. You'll be able to register each semester and choose your classes, check your grades, see professor notes and lectures, submit homework assignments or even exams, and collaborate with other students on projects. You should also be aware of more technical resources you can access such as web page hosting services for students and network sharing resources like the Windows Active Directory where students and faculty can share files and folders on their computer over the network.

While computer networks provide many valuable features, they can also provide hazards, so safety and security are of paramount importance. This has become an only greater problem over time.

Computer safety and security

Computer security issues have existed for decades, but now the problem is much more acute. Before, all you would lose was your data. Now you can have your bank accounts emptied, identity stolen, and private information publicly distributed. There are several basic steps you can take from the beginning to secure yourself. Then we can show more advanced tactics.

First and foremost is you must purchase a good antivirus program. There are many common packages from firms like Symantec, McAfee, or Kaspersky. Commonly these packages include not only antivirus protection but system maintenance and backup programs as well. These will automatically update over time and are usually subscription based, so they must be renewed once a year. Often, new computers will include these programs and a year's subscription. If not, you should purchase and install these as soon as you turn your computer on for the first time and definitely before using the Internet.

However essential antivirus programs are, they are often only a first line of defense. Another problem is spyware, programs that you often unknowingly get on your computer from websites you visit that track your behavior and report it back to its source. All antivirus programs have spyware protection as well but there are also free programs that are a good complement to antivirus programs to root out spyware. At download.com the two best are Lavasoft AdAware and Malwarebytes Anti-Malware. These and your antivirus program can be set up to run on regular intervals such as late at night to ensure regular scanning.

Being smart will help keep viruses from being an issue. For example, be careful when sharing USB keys. If someone's laptop is not properly protected, it could be infected. Your antivirus software may or may not pick up the infection before it is passed to you. This doesn't mean being paranoid—in work groups people often use USB sticks to share files. You often have to use public computers and you can use a USB key but follow a few steps. First, make sure the last person logged out and if not reboot the computer and log back in. Second, always scan the files and your USB key before you remove it when you are done. Finally, you may look for tips online about securing the USB key from viruses. There is a file on USB keys called autorun.inf that viruses use to infect other computers from a USB key and you may want to disable this.

Never use a USB key that you find and are not sure who it belongs to. Hand it in to the lost and found or the IT department. USB or disk viruses (known as boot sector viruses) are a lot less common since email and the Internet are now the preferred ways to spread viruses. It still pays to be safe though.

A primary source of viruses and trojans has increasingly been email. You'll receive emails from unknown parties or even friends with generic messages and file attachments like Word documents, zip files, or Internet links. Never open an attachment in an unsolicited email from an unknown person, especially if the message text seems extremely generic. In 'phishing' schemes you'll receive an email that looks just like one from your bank or school asking you to go to a site and enter your username and password. As regular policy no bank will do this. If you ever have a doubt, call the toll-free number on the official bank website (not the one from the email) to confirm the veracity of these emails. Clicking on the links in malicious emails will often install software on the computer to allow thieves to steal your data, remote control your computer, or even use it as an intermediary to commit a crime. Campus IT will often send alerts on these when they become prevalent, so pay attention.

Protecting your account security is paramount. This includes not only username and password for the school system but also webmail such as Gmail, Facebook, and iTunes. Never distribute these passwords to anyone. There are many ways to manage them from keeping a (secure and hidden) list of your passwords or using online third-party password managers like LastPass. Paper lists have the risk of being stolen or compromised. Third-party password managers can be hacked as well but usually have industrial strength protection. There are even iPhone apps like Datavault and mSecure that act as password managers. What you should not do is keep a file on your computer with all your passwords, even if it is a password protected Word or Excel file. These can easily be stolen and hacked.

What also helps is having tiers of passwords. For example, for important things like your bank, school account, Gmail, or Facebook, you should have different passwords for each containing numbers, letters, and symbols. For more minor things such as various online sites that aren't really important, you can share a password or passwords for many of them. These can be relatively simple and easy to remember. Make sure none of these minor sites has your credit card information though. This does mean that compromising one can compromise all of them but if they are non-essential resources, there's less of an issue.

Never reuse a password from an online social networking site like Facebook or email like Gmail on another account. These are the most often targeted by thieves and hackers and typically once they have one, they can find the username for others and hack those as well if you share passwords. One thing I often do is maintain two or three email accounts. One is my primary, which is used for important communication, another is secondary and used for mailing lists, site registrations, and for giving to people I don't know to prevent spam and email stalking, and a final one is used in case I ever need to send something anonymously. This is not for illegal activity or threats but for posting on message boards, letters to parties I don't want tracking my activity via searching my email address in Google, etc.

It's often safer not to log into accounts such as banking or even Facebook from public computers. Though campus computers are often secured pretty well, they are public and if a program called a keystroke logger is installed by a malicious party, it can track your keystrokes and thus obtain password information. Remember, it takes only one infected party to spread a virus to one or multiple computers.

If you ever find any type of account compromised, contact the customer service and technical support group of that service immediately to have it deactivated before more mischief can be caused. Also, alert any key people your account is hacked and to not trust any messages from it. To prevent account theft, you can often have a backup email or phone number that Gmail, Facebook, and others can use to verify your identity and restore your account.

A final thing to remember is to frequently back up your computer. It's no understatement that your life will soon be on your computer, and having a hard drive failure or theft could set you back weeks or months. Backing up your information is easy and there are several options depending on your comfort level, desire for control, and cost. The oldest and still likely most common method of backup is a spare external hard drive. You can back up the computer yourself by just copying over important folders regularly to help protect valuable personal information. This requires discipline though to do on a frequent schedule. If you do backup to an external hard drive, don't carry it with you in your computer bag. If the bag is stolen you lose both your computer and backup. Better to leave it in a safe place in your dorm room or apartment. Using a software program or online service such as Mozy can be more convenient since it's automated and easily accessible.

Online privacy

Closely related to security is online privacy. The large-scale searchability and long-term permanency of the Internet allow massive amounts of previously private information to be revealed. Embarrassing things you reveal online during college may never go away and could be easy to find decades from now. Therefore, you should be cautious of the type and volume of personal information you place on the Internet.

Personal private information is typically not divulged when people think of the actual consequences. In fact, it can be given out with seemingly innocuous activities such as mailing lists. Private information you reveal can range from your name and address, your hobbies and habits, relationships, political opinions, and financial information. Again, this is a topic that could merit its own book but here we'll discuss several key things you must know about online privacy to keep your personal information safe.

Email privacy

Email is not private, unless it's encrypted, and this is typically not the case. How so? Part of this involves the nature of the Internet where emails and files are broken up into small pieces called packets and routed through different computers to their final destination. Eavesdroppers or anyone who can compromise the recipient's email account or their email provider can see your emails. So what does this mean? Never send hypersensitive information like your credit card numbers, social security numbers, passport numbers, or important passwords over email.

Even if you aren't hacked, you should be aware that many webmail systems like Gmail mine your emails and their details as a way to target ads towards you. Now that Google has united their privacy policies, the information from Gmail will be combined with that from YouTube, searches, Google Phone, etc. to profile you and sell ads. If this is a problem for you, you may want to have your email separate from where you search. So if you search with Google you can use Hotmail. This is a more extreme measure but just know that your privacy is more consistently being violated in the name of advertising and profiling.

One other issue regarding emails is that some can become public. Most notably are emails to mailing lists. Often, these mailing list archives end up being posted online and publicly searchable.

Anything you say embarrassing or inflammatory could then become a matter of public knowledge.

Basic identifiers: Internet Protocol (IP) addresses and Media Access Control (MAC) addresses

You and your activity can be tracked by several key markers. On controlled systems like campus networks, this can be your username or email. More commonly used are IP addresses and MAC addresses. IP addresses are unique numerical addresses used to identify a computer on the Internet. The traditional IP addresses, IP version 4 (IPv4) are combinations of four numbers between 0 and 255. For example, 152.8.104.106 is the unique IP address for the library website of North Carolina A&T. Newer IP addresses in IPv6 will be even longer having 8 groups of digits. Every computer connected to the Internet, including devices like printers, has an IP address. Some of these are fixed or 'static' and follow the computer wherever it goes. Others are 'dynamic' and a different one is assigned whenever the computer connects to the network. Either way, these IP addresses are a pointer to your computer whenever you do lots of activities such as log in to any website, online-based email, or do almost anything else. This can be used to track you and your activity by websites, network administrators, and anyone in between.

MAC addresses are similar but much more intrinsic to your computer. A MAC address is a numerical identifier on network interfaces such as Ethernet network cards and wireless network cards you use for Wi-Fi. These are matched with an IP address by the network and can be used to tie an IP address directly to your computer.

Most networks have tools called packet sniffers that monitor the traffic by IP addresses on the network. Sometimes records are kept for security or network analysis purposes. I will not get any more technical, but this information is to demonstrate to you that what you do online: be it browsing websites, sending personal information, downloading files from P2P services and file sharing sites, and even chatting on instant messenger can be tracked.

How can you avoid eavesdropping on your online activities? One way is to use proxy servers. Proxy servers are servers that sit between the source (you) and your destination website and can allow you to surf the web without compromising your privacy since from the perspective of the college network and the destination web site, all data flows to the proxy server. However, some proxy servers are transparent, so your traffic is not completely hidden, or could even be eavesdropping themselves, so this method is not foolproof. There are also many products on the market, both free and for pay, that can encrypt your data and reroute your traffic to avoid detection. While this won't hide your IP address from the network you connect through, it can protect your traffic contents and their destination. The basic mechanism is that these services use intermediate router(s) to hide the origin and destination of the packet from the destination and origin computer networks and also encrypt the data in the packets so that their contents cannot be viewed by a third party.

A popular and free software tool that does this is Tor, which uses a massive network of routers and encryption to hide the packet destination and source from eavesdropping. Tor is often used in foreign countries where Internet monitoring and censorship by government agencies is pervasive. A pay version of this type of service is offered by Anonymizer, which uses its own set of servers and encrypts your traffic. On average it costs about one hundred dollars per year but can give you online privacy with little change in speed or network performance.

Web browsers

Web browsing can offer another unwanted intrusion into your privacy through cookies and web-based malware (malicious programs) exploits against browsers. Most websites these days install cookies on your machine when you visit them. Cookies are small text files that contain information, often about your browsing activities and preferences, on your hard drive. These can reveal information to other websites, not just the one that installed the cookie. There is also programmed code most websites use called scripts that while usually harmless can also attack the browser or computer to install malware. There is software to deal with scripts, such as NoScript for Mozilla Firefox, which allows you to choose whether you let a site execute scripts. It can make browsing a bit more difficult but eliminates the chance a malicious site can automatically launch code against your computer.

These cookies are often cleaned by modern antivirus utilities. You can also delete them through options on any browser. Granted, stored information like shopping cart contents and sites where you stayed logged into will disappear. Another privacy breach is that all browsers store site browsing history of sites you have visited and searches you have performed on websites like Google. They also store, with your permission, usernames and passwords. One of my favorite browsers, Mozilla Firefox, has a private browsing option that lets you browse without the fear of any history and the deletion of cookies once browsing sessions have ended. Another option can be using encrypted links on all websites possible. You know if a website is encrypted if you see a 'https' in its address instead of 'http'. The Electronic Frontier Foundation has a free Firefox add-on called Https Everywhere that allows your browser to encrypt the website whenever possible. Again it's up to you how much of this you want to do, but I would recommend that you delete your history, cookies and all, at least once a week. It not only protects personal information but makes your browser run faster.

One final note is that when you search on a search engine where you're logged in, this information can and will be used to sell you advertisements, often on the email service. A prime example is Google where searching while logged in adds to your overall profile. Typically I log out of Google before doing a search.

Social networking

Yes, everyone seems to use Facebook. It's a great tool for communication, though it should definitely not be your primary tool. There have been recent rafts of problems with privacy in Facebook, however. That ranges from privacy settings that make your details visible to any stranger if you aren't careful to people hijacking your account for malicious purposes. Often the worst breaches of privacy are things you do or say on Facebook.

A good guide to read is from the site Lifehacker which has the "The Always Up-to-Date Guide to Managing Your Facebook Privacy." It is a good guide to Facebook privacy settings to allow you to carefully tailor who can see what about you. You can control your privacy through two main methods on Facebook: managing your privacy settings so others don't see your personal posts and pictures or don't post super private information on Facebook. The latter is always the most secure since if Facebook changes the rules, or if you piss someone off, you have to go through the motions to change it all again. You can control what you post on Facebook and who tags you in photos, and I suggest you use that power as your first line of defense to protect your privacy online. Facebook keeps records on everything you do and tracks whose profile pages you visit and who you communicate with so you're opening yourself up a bit no matter what you do. Let's admit it: Mark Zuckerberg is a great guy, but Facebook is a business. The best description of its business model that I've ever heard is that it buys your privacy at a discount and sells it (to advertisers) for a premium. Again, this isn't a call for paranoia, just be aware.

Your information on Facebook can be used by jealous exes, stalkers, and criminals who try to use your personal information to get you or others to divulge important details they can capitalize on such as financial information. The same goes for other sites like LinkedIn, which shows your full school and professional information, so always be careful what you put out there. No amount of privacy settings can save you from stupidity.

Instant messaging, outside of site platforms like Facebook, is generally more secure but again it isn't private. Also, many worms try to spread through instant messaging networks by hacking one account and sending the entire buddy list a dummy message with a link that takes you to a malicious website. I know you may be rolling your eyes at this but trust me, the crooks never sleep and get more inventive all the time.

A final new phenomena (or threat) in this area are college gossip forums. Started a few years ago by a site called JuicyCampus.com and later continued by others like College ACB, people are allowed to post anonymous gossip, often malicious, about their classmates for the world to read. I would not recommend using these sites or even believing half of their information since someone posting something malicious often has an agenda, however you should make sure you watch to see if your name is often being dragged through the mud. If so, there are ways to contact the administrators of the site to remove the offensive or slanderous posts and block the IP address that posted it. One easy way to track your name online is to set up a Google Alert with your name. Google will then email you every time a new page or news article with your name pops up.

Peer-to-peer (P2P) networks and filesharing

This is where I give my old man back in the day talk. Back in the day I didn't walk five miles through snow uphill to get to school, but sharing MP3s was a lot harder. We didn't have P2P until roughly my junior year when Napster came on the scene, so before that you had to visit search engines for FTP servers people set up on their own computers. There was a trade system once you logged in: for every song you downloaded you had to upload one or more new ones. That way their library expanded and they kept the freeloaders off. I had some dorm mates in computer engineering who built an MP3 player. It was the size of a toaster. Nowadays kids all have it easy.

P2P is a system where you use software to share files between a pair of computers without relying on a server (master computer) in-between. There are dozens of P2P software packages and many like eMule/eDonkey and Bitorrent have massive user bases. Everything seems easy and anonymous, right? Well, no. As before, your IP is always there. Though the Motion Picture Association of America (MPAA) and the Recording Industry Association of America (RIAA), which represent the film and music industries respectively, are not suing individuals like they did right when P2P file sharing became big, you are not necessarily anonymous. You can encrypt Bitorrent traffic, but the computers you download from will have your IP. I have yet to hear about huge privacy implications from P2P. Since the lawsuits are not as prevalent and many schools will not hand over IP logs, it's likely there may not even be legal culpability. Like all things, use with caution.

File downloading sites also record IP information, but the authorities usually focus on shutting down the sites and not prosecuting individual users. The recent takedown of Megaupload has put a bit of a chill on the whole industry, though it's likely that the schemes will just migrate to countries where they are beyond the long arm of law enforcement. If you have IP anonymizers like Anonymizer though the tracing won't be an issue. Never use a strange or rarely known file sharing site. If you have doubts, search it in Google with the term "+spyware." There was a Russian site a couple of years back that returned download results for any keyword, no matter how nonsensical, and that convinced people to set up payment for faster download to find out it was really a credit card stealing scam.

In all this, realize downloading MP3s and movies without payment is illegal, and if your computer is ever seized, this can be used to prosecute you to the full extent of the law. In the age of Netflix and iTunes, I really have not had a need to bootleg stuff, and I think digital content delivery will be even cheaper and faster in the future.

Other devices: smartphones, tablets, etc.

Phones now have more processing power than the desktop I had in college, and tablets have opened a whole new world of interactivity. The problem is these are prime targets for thieves. For this reason, I keep only minimal private information on my cell phone and never allow the phone browser to save my passwords. In addition, realize there is a lot of software out there that tracks your phone browsing and calling habits, once again, to sell advertising. There was a lot of uproar over one piece of software called CarrierIQ that reported user behavior to cell phone providers. This was bad but I know from a reliable source in the security industry that CarrierIQ was only one, and not the worst, out of many.

Apple and Google will probably mine your behavior and location (via GPS) on iPhones and Android phones respectively for some sort of user data collection. Just realize that your phone is creating a profile of who you call, what you like, and other information, so be careful what you do on it and what you use it for.

Tablets are the new craze and whether it is from Apple, Samsung, or Amazon you may want to look into buying one. For one, eBooks are increasingly popular and a tablet like an Amazon Kindle is always more convenient to carry than a massive book. Second, textbooks now have cheaper eBook versions that may save you money. Finally, some people like tablets to the point they are replacing their laptops. I personally would not go this far but if you are not a laptop power user, maybe you will use your tablet much more.

Buying a tablet is similar to buying a smartphone. You choose between an Apple product, an Android based one, or a Microsoft based one. You also use a cell phone provider if you want Internet outside of Wi-Fi coverage areas. If you do buy a tablet, make sure you know what you want to use it for so it won't collect dust in the corner. If only for eBooks, you may not need a high-priced iPad. Do your research and choose accordingly.

Final notes-other technology

We have covered most of your technology needs in this chapter. There are a few other things, mostly older technology, you'll have to consider. Due to the rise of cell phones, not all campuses give landline service and some make you pay for it. You don't have to have a landline, but I like to do so as a backup. People can also call if I don't want to give out my cell phone. Also, in an emergency, the cell towers may be overloaded as they often are during natural disasters or events like 9/11. These landlines may gradually disappear though.

It's your choice whether to get a TV and what kind, but since most new computers have flatscreen monitor options and BluRay players, it may not be necessary. You can even buy cards for desktops to allow you to plug in and access cable. Cable providers offer video-on-demand online, and there's Netflix streaming, so in all honesty, if I were in college again I wouldn't feel pressed to buy a TV. For larger screens and surround sound though, nothing beats getting a good TV, so evaluate your needs and buy accordingly.

Conclusion

Technology is extremely important in college, and there's no better time in life to find out about the latest and greatest in cutting-edge technology. You should evaluate your needs and purchase technology accordingly. I would not recommend used computers as technology changes fast and you want to try to prevent having to upgrade later. Privacy and security are extremely important and while they may seem a burden at first, once you adopt good habits you can keep yourself safe without much effort

Chapter 11
Career

Success runs in our race.
—George Fraser

College is fun, but at the back of our minds we all know it's preparing us for life ahead. Many of the preparations are academic, others are social, but one that becomes more prominent as you approach senior year is career. It's funny that you've been asked all of your life what you want to be when you grow up and now you are grown up and need to be somebody. You have many opportunities to make your mark and find your dream job, but you also face daunting challenges. You are likely graduating into the worst U.S. economy since the Great Depression, and it's likely to continue in this rut for some time. A college degree, once a guarantee of a job, is now a common commodity. Roughly, college degrees are equivalent to what high school degrees were fifty years ago—everyone has them, and they're not necessarily a differentiator. Going to a higher ranked school may help, but many people have seen the world through ivy-tinted glasses, only to see their hopes dashed upon graduation.

Getting a job, or even more, a particular type of job, is no guarantee. I wouldn't say there's a sure-fire method in these troubled times. However, knowing what you're up against and how to best prepare yourself will be the focus of this chapter. I apologize for starting out so negatively. The focus of this chapter is largely positive in that it helps you know what to do and how to prepare to land a great job at graduation. However, preparing for the worst and getting the best is always a preferred strategy than relying on fantasy or wishful thinking to generate results.

Preparation: prepare early, prepare often

If you start thinking about the job and career game the fall or spring of senior year, you're already behind the eight ball. Like many things in life, preparation is essential and the entire career landscape and interview process can take months to understand. If you start in September of your senior year and take three months to understand the whole system, how many interviews or chances have you squandered? Remember, the working world, unlike school, is usually rolling admissions so everything is first come, first served. There are some exceptions like consulting, investment banking, or accounting firms that hire in classes but even those start early.

Even if you're not a senior and only looking for internships, you shouldn't wait until the spring semester, which is the typical recruiting and interviewing season for internship positions. Again the logic is the same, and in a competitive environment, you must work to get ahead of the crowd, not rush in at the same time with them.

One of the easiest ways to get a college student to look like a deer in the headlights is to ask the simple question: where do you want to work after graduation? Students destined for graduate schools such as law and medicine have easy answers, but others may be unsure. You may be happy to take any job that comes your way. However, this is not the best way to start a job search or perform an interview. If you have an ideal job, that is great, but if not, you need to evaluate your skills and interests and get in contact with your career office.

Your first visit to the career office can be in your sophomore or junior year. You should set up a private appointment with a counselor, not just drop in. In setting up the appointment, you should give the counselor a clear idea of your background, skills, aspirations, and what kind of career guidance you want. In addition, you should come to the first meeting with a résumé. It does not have to be perfect, but you're bringing it primarily for feedback. You'll need someone to help you go over your résumé several times to perfect it, including having the right kind of information, having the right language, and being in the right format and length.

During your meeting you should ask for an assessment of likely careers, their skills, and your marketability in those fields. For every career you're interested in, you should ask if you can find an alumni contact who's working in that field. This is a person you can contact to ask more in-depth questions and possibly meet. This can be a valuable networking opportunity. In addition, as stated in Chapter 3 on finance, for every industry or career you're interested in, you should look up its industry association. If you're very interested, join the association as a student member and subscribe to its magazine to learn more about the industry. If the membership fee is high, write an officer of the organization directly and ask for a discount as an undergraduate. You may get in for free. This can help you see if you like it as well as gain valuable knowledge for interviews. Some associations have local chapter meetings. If so, you should attend and network if at all possible.

Network, Network, Network

Getting into the right career will take more than just submissions to a job website. Usually, these are not answered. The real champions of the job search use networking. Remember, it's not what you know but who you know that makes you successful. For networking you need a few major things. First, a set of business cards. These can state your name and your email, your school, major, graduation date, and career options for which you are looking. Second, you need an elevator pitch. This is a thirty-second speech that talks about you, your background, your strengths, and what you are looking for. If you have doubts about it, practice it with one of the counselors in the career office. A great book about networking is *Success Runs in Our Race* by George Fraser. I definitely recommend you read this before plunging headlong into the networking game.

If you're serious about networking, have some business cards on you at all times because you never know where you'll meet someone to network with, be it on a bus, in an airport, or in a restaurant. I met a business contact once through his wife working in a tourist store in southern Germany! Good thing I had plenty of cards on hand.

You should look for targeted networking opportunities. As I mentioned above, local meetings of industry groups are great places to network. It also helps learn a lot about a job or industry. If

you're really ambitious, going to the national conference for the industry organization can make you
great contacts and greatly increase the chance of
landing a job. That's actually how I landed my first
job out of grad school. Use the student angle to
possibly get free admittance to the conference
since the registration fees are often high. Remember, many great jobs aren't posted and can only be
found through networking. Other good organizations to network at are local organizations like the
Rotary clubs or other business groups, local Black
organizations like 100 Black Men or fraternity
events, college or graduate school conferences, and
on the golf course.

The key thing about networking is you have to
be willing to talk to people and have interesting
conversations. Don't network with only a narrow
purpose in mind and jump from person to person
to find what you want. Talk to people and get to
know them and let them get to know you. You may
find many hidden opportunities or contacts you
would have otherwise never considered. Also,
don't just network with who is considered elite.
Meeting and greeting people from all walks of life
is essential. Think about it: do you know the name
of your janitor at your dorm? Why not? They may
be someone great to talk to and get to know.

Technology has helped networking immensely.
The rise of LinkedIn and many other similar networking sites has made it exponentially easier to
search for and connect with people. A great tactic
to communicate with someone at a company is to
find their profile on LinkedIn and then send them
an email. You can do this through LinkedIn InMail
though you have to be a subscriber. Another meth-

od is to search for their name and company on Google to find their email address if you are not a close contact on LinkedIn. A lot of company email addresses are in the format firstname.lastname@companyname.com. You can search for the person's name and drop them a line directly, which is often much better than trying to use the résumé dump on their website.

Career fairs are also a great contact place but can be huge and intimidating. Get a list of the companies and go to the ones you're interested in first. Make sure you have a copy of your résumé to leave with them. Also, don't limit yourself to career fairs in your school or town but look at surrounding schools or towns as well. Get business cards of the people you meet and be sure to follow up with them by email later that day while you are still on their mind. This may help you get called in for an interview.

Finally, as stated before, career mentors can be crucial. Often the best way to find them is through the career office's alumni services group. The office can hook you up with a great mentor. Also, some of the industry organizations mentioned before, professors, or guest speakers who come to the university can be great mentors or hook you up with mentors. Jump at the chance to get a mentor if you're interested in a field since it can make all the difference between searching fruitlessly or being guided to a job.

Internships

A vital part of your college career can be an internship where you work at a company for a summer or sometimes during winter break. These can be great work experiences to see what you like, improve your résumé, or earn money on the side. Internships often have interviews in the spring semester so you need to keep your eye out for when the companies are coming on campus to interview.

An important part of the internship search is once again, early preparation. Many people wander aimlessly at college career fairs looking at whomever seems to have the best display, coolest representatives, or brand name recognition. This can be a strategy, but you need to stand out from the crowd in today's competitive environment.

Internships also have their own rhyme or reason. Some in competitive fields like media are unpaid. Others pay competitive salaries. If you're interested in interning at a company it could help if you could find someone who has worked there before. For the most common companies, there may be someone visiting on campus who's open to talking to you. Otherwise, the career office or the company itself will propose the name of someone for you to talk to.

There are also programs that place you into internships. There are organizations such as INROADS which was created for this purpose to help minorities find internships. As an alum, I highly recommend INROADS as a wonderful organization that can get you into good opportunities. There is also a similar organization focused on investment banking called SEO.

For the most competitive internships like those in media or congressional interns the competition is high and you need to talk to multiple people ahead of time to see what they are looking for. In these situations grades are often not enough, and essays, contacts, grueling interviews and other such measures may be what's necessary to put you ahead of the pack.

When internships aren't available, sometimes there's something called shadowing where you can tag along (unpaid) at a job to find out what it's like. These can be great opportunities to gauge career interests as well as build contacts.

When you get an internship, you need to be on your A game. You must perform since this may be the best chance to land a job post-graduation. That means following all the rules, arriving on time, understanding corporate etiquette and doing a good job. Some people look at interns as a waste of money or a token, so everything bad you do can be magnified. If you do well and the company is willing, you may come to campus your senior year with a job in hand.

Job interviews

You've submitted your résumé, got an email or call back, and been invited to an interview. What now? Interviews can be tough, but they're often the deciding factor between having a job or not, regardless of your credentials. Therefore, you must be ready.

First is attire. Always wear a business suit and tie to an interview, regardless of the company's typical attire. Most companies now do business casual, but that still doesn't allow you to dress down for an interview. Make sure it's dry cleaned before you go, and if you're traveling, make sure you have everything (suit jacket, pants, shirt, tie, belt, shoes, socks) before you leave. Also, you may want to consider a haircut and shaving if that's not a regular thing. You can have a beard but it's best to have it trimmed by a barber to look good.

There's a lot of controversy about hair, piercings, etc., and the workplace. I'm all for individualism, but you need to assume conservative unless you know otherwise. Going into an interview you should probably remove any piercings, even those in your ear. I know these days men and earrings are not as big a deal, but you don't know how the interviewer will see you. The earring won't get lonely for an hour, so leave it at home. Also cover up any tattoos, especially on your neck (which is another good reason for suit collars). If you wear dreadlocks and want to keep them, make sure they are not unkempt. Finally, speak in as clear, proper English as possible. Everyone, including me, speaks vernacular around their friends but there are those who will incorrectly judge you if you don't speak standard English. Dispense of the slang and abbreviations in the interview. Finally, treat the interviewer like the professional he or she is. If it's a girl, don't flirt with her. If it's a guy, keep jokes clean and to a minimum unless they initiate them. You never know what offends people.

There are several types of interviews you may encounter. Most common is the behavioral interview, which asks you questions about yourself, your skills, and why you want the job. This is what people typically think of as an interview. For a behavioral interview, it's best to think of some common questions in advance. Common questions include your interests, what you think your key strengths and weaknesses are, your goals in life, and what you like about the company.

Case study interviews involve the interviewer presenting a hypothetical situation, such as a business situation, and asking you to think through the problem and offer a solution. These are common with consulting firms, sometimes banks, and other high-end service companies. These are best prepared for through practice. There are some good case interview books such as the one published by *The Vault*. If you purchase it you can get a friend to practice interview you with the guide. Also, some career centers or companies hold mock case interviews to help interviewees prepare.

For case interviews, it's best to come with a pen and paper to write down the key facts the interviewer gives. Then you need to think about how these facts relate to each other and the problem being addressed. Remember you can ask questions. When you answer, talk the interviewer through the logic of your answer in order to make sure you both understand and agree with it. The interviewer may be coy about divulging important information but at least they'll know where you're coming from.

The rarest types of interviews are psychological interviews where you'll be asked personal questions that are supposed to reveal your psychological makeup. This may include a personality test like the Myers-Briggs or even a pseudo-IQ test. These are very rare though for someone at the level of a college student.

In an interview, there are several make-or-break things that haven't been addressed above. First, never, ever lie. Not on your résumé, not about your background, and not in answering the questions. If they catch the lie, you're done. If they don't, you'll have to live in fear of being discovered and subsequently fired. Never add experience to your résumé you didn't have. Résumé fraud scandals have been pervasive lately at all levels of many companies and even schools!

Next, make sure you research the company well before you get to the interview. This can involve the company website, annual reports, news on the company from news aggregators like Google News, and newspapers like the *Wall Street Journal* or *Financial Times*. Speaking of these two newspapers, if you're interested in business, it's best you start at least looking at the headlines and main stories several times a week to keep up with the business world. Often schools subscribe to these electronically and you can read from your dorm room.

After the interview, ask the interviewer for honest feedback, thank him or her, and that *same day* write a thank you letter to the interviewer for spending the time interviewing you. Don't pester the interviewer days after the interview to see if you made it. Typically, I wait two weeks. If they want to contact you, they usually will in due course. Badgering them isn't going to help. Finally, never retaliate or send a hostile email or place a phone call if you don't get a job. No matter how you feel, again thank them and ask what you could have done better. It never pays to burn bridges.

And if at first you fail...

You will likely have many interviews and more than a few failures before you land a job. One of the most important things is to never get discouraged. It does hurt one's self-esteem and confidence to get turned down again and again, but it's important that you learn from each experience and never give up. As graduation approaches, you may get increasingly nervous if you haven't landed anything. Ignore the peer pressure or gloating by friends at their great post-graduation prospects. Make sure you ask the career office to continue supporting you, even post-graduation. I actually got the best job I ever had after I had graduated from grad school, so it pays to not give up, especially if you have a good (and realistic) idea of what you want.

In addition, you may want to look beyond the typical premier jobs and cities to recognize many good opportunities off the beaten path. Everyone wants to work in New York or Atlanta and for the big-name prestigious companies. This can be good but it can be very limiting if that's all you're looking for. These are great places and thus are very competitive. You shouldn't shy from competition, that's hardly what I'm proposing, but there are often great jobs that go begging for takers from lesser known companies or in lesser known regions. You're young and are likely very flexible. This can be a time to travel and find a good job in a city you may not have originally considered. I'm not saying you have to go totally off the map but if you reject a job because it's in Omaha or Santa Fe you may be cutting yourself off from some great opportunities.

The same goes for companies. There are some massive corporations that are essential to our economy but are often unknown because they don't sell directly to consumers or they make 'boring' products. They can be great opportunities for both career enrichment and learning about business in general. They may also offer greater opportunities than the oversubscribed firms that everyone runs to.

Another option people don't often think of are Black-owned firms. There are many Black-owned businesses that struggle to find good people to help push the firm forward. A good source to find these is the annual *Black Enterprise 100* that lists the country's top Black businesses. It would allow you to advance your career and help create great Black businesses in one fell swoop.

You should even be flexible about looking abroad if that's where the opportunity lies. If you've already studied abroad you know how great the world can be. We live in an age where the United States no longer has a monopoly on the greatest jobs. Look over the horizon and there may be opportunities you don't expect.

Despite setbacks, it's important that you keep looking for a job. Giving up only guarantees you won't get one. The loans will come due and your self-respect will demand you try to at least help make ends meet. This is a tough time for everyone, so keep your head up and keep pressing on.

Alternative options

If the job just isn't there, there are other options. One is non-profit work. This can range from working for low pay with a non-profit relevant to your career experience to the Peace Corps to missionary work. Often, jobs as an English teacher are available in many countries in Asia or Latin America. By local salary standards, they can pay decently and offer a great learning experience. If you have loans though, these options may not leave you much money on the side after those are taken care of.

Entrepreneurship is a perennial option that many should consider. There are many books out there on starting your own business, and if you have a good idea, it could be worth a try. If you do start a business, you must remember to understand the market you are selling to and make sure the opportunity is there, know how to write a competent business plan to attract investors or potential partners, and finally find ways to raise capital which often come from friends or family. Try to limit as much as possible using your own money by either receiving loans from others or offering them an equity stake in your business.

Entrepreneurship can be rewarding, but also very risky. You're your own boss but have to understand the laws of incorporation, business, sales and payroll taxes, and basic accounting. You'll likely work more than forty hours a week if you're serious and have to provide your own health insurance. If you think this is for you, I would suggest picking up some good books on the subject and start subscribing to magazines like *Inc.*, *Entrepreneur*, or *FastCompany* to get the tips and begin talking to other entrepreneurs on web forums, local business incubators, and meetings like the Rotary Club.

Conclusion

The career search is an extremely important part of your college experience. It's vital that you start early and get all the support you can upfront in order to stand out to potential employers. Remember that contacts are key. Start making these the moment you start on campus if possible. Hopefully you'll land your dream job on the first try, but if not, don't be snobby. Taking a job that you may not think is the best can allow you to get experience to get a better job later. Holding out for the perfect job is like holding out for the perfect girl: it probably doesn't exist and you pass up many nice ones while you are being obstinate. If you have to pay the bills and are just starting out, it may pay to try out a job you initially don't think much of. If you do, work hard and squeeze all the experience and knowledge you want out of it and you may surprise yourself at what you can accomplish.

Concluding Remarks

Well, I guess it's time for me to quiet down and let you go about your business. You are embarking on what will probably be the most enjoyable and enriching time of your life. There will be ups and downs and there will be great triumphs as well as great disappointments. I hope you will find the advice in this book helpful in navigating the great challenge lying before you.

Despite some of the stern advice and gloom and doom statistics, I think the odds are on your side. The fact that you are even where you are in life shows you have the brains, mettle, and drive to accomplish your goals in college. Lack of focus or financial means sink far more people in college than do failure despite honest effort and hard work. You should seize every opportunity before you and make the best effort to be a star in everything. Some people will judge you whether because you are a Black male, where you came from, or how audacious your dreams might be. Eleanor Roosevelt once eloquently said, "no one can make you feel inferior without your consent," so do not become your own worst enemy and allow yourself to overshadow your strengths and past accomplishments with doubts and insecurities.

When you look back on these years, you will want to feel a sense not only of accomplishment but of having fun, making friends for life, and perhaps even finding a life partner. You may also look back on who you were in high school or freshman year and smile or cringe at the immaturities you exhibited. But remember, college is a period of growth like no other and it would be surprising indeed if you left the same person as you came in. On the cover of this book is a piece by Kameel J. Mateen called, "Still I Rise." It invokes much of what I see as an idealized college student mastering great books of knowledge and shooting for the stars. Whatever your dream is, and however it might change, if this book was able to help you in even a small measure, it has accomplished its mission.

About the Author

R. (Reginald) D. Smith originally hails from Decatur, GA. He studied at the University of Virginia in Charlottesville, VA where he received a B.S. in Commerce and completed the requirements for a B.A. in physics (UVA does not award double majors). He subsequently studied his MBA, concentrating in supply chain and operations at the Sloan School of Management at the Massachusetts Institute of Technology (MIT). Enjoying global business and culture, he has traveled and worked around the world including China, Brazil, and Europe. Practicing what he preached, he learned Mandarin Chinese, Brazilian Portuguese, and Spanish while in school or on various assignments abroad. He will always cherish his college years at Thomas Jefferson's university and the springboard it gave him for his entire life.

Index

Academics
    Add/drop, 29-30
    Course load, 26-27
    Dishonesty, 49-52
    Foreign languages, 60-61
    Freshmen, 54-55
    Labs, 29-30
    Learning, 20-23
    Libraries, 24-26
    Majors, 32-35
    Remedial classes, 31
    Study habits, 40-49
    TA sessions, 28, 39-40
Alcohol, 130, 148, 151-155, 173, 234
Bikes, 226-228
Books (buying), 35-37
Career
    Internships, 276-278
    Interviews, 278-281
    Preparation, 272-274
    Networking, 274-276
Cars, 66, 154-155, 222-226
Class Issues, 238-241

Cults (dangers of), 199-203
Drugs
    Financial aid, 80-81
    Health dangers, 166-169
EdCon levels, 41-43
Engineering Majors, 55-58
Entrepreneurship, 14, 91-93, 284
Extracurriculars
    Athletics, 203-204
    Black professional groups, 192
    Ethnic organizations, 189-191
    Faith, 197-199
    Leadership, 193-195
    Student Government, 186-187
    Student Groups, 187-189
Extremist Groups, 195-196
Finances
    Basics, 66-69
    Credit cards, 84-87
    Grants, 69-70
    Loans (federal), 71-73

Loans (private), 73-78

Loans (state), 73

Making money, 88-93

Health

Diet, 140-145

Depression, 158-160

Exercise, 145-146

Illness, 148-151

Mental, 155-160

Pregnancy, 164-166

Sleep, 146-148

STDs, 160-164

Suicide, 159-160

Journal (for college), 14-18

Pre-Med, 58-59

Pre-Law, 58-59

Pregnancy, 164-166

Relationships

Faculty, 131-134

Friends, 101-106

Interracial, 121-124

Romantic, 106-131

Roommates, 98-101

Safety, 128-131

Race issues, 232-238

Rape, 129-130, 155

Safety

Basics, 170-172

Disasters, 182-183

Driving, 225-226

Firearms, 181-182

Law enforcement, 174-181

Parties, 172-174

Relationships, 128-131

Science Majors, 55-58

Sex, 118-121, 160-165

Study Abroad

Friends, 211-212

Preparation, 209-210

Scholarships, 208-209

Women, 215-219

Working, 212-214

Statistics (Black men in college), 9-10, 32

Technology

Awareness, 244-245

Buying a computer, 245-249, 266-267

IP & MAC address,

P2P software, 260, 265-266

Privacy, 257-261

Safety, 266-267

Software, 249-251

Transferring Schools, 62-63

Made in the USA
Charleston, SC
17 February 2013